To Melissa,
I wish you the smiles in the world! Hope you get a few here...

♡

Than
2005

A GATHERING OF POETS

AN ANTHOLOGY OF
POETRY
ART
PHOTOGRAPHY

**CREATED BY THE POETRY WORKSHOP
OF
THE FREDERICKSBURG CENTER FOR THE CREATIVE ARTS**

WORKSHOP CHAIRPERSON: CHARLOTTE GARRETT

MEMBERS

**ANNE FLYTHE
CHARLOTTE GARRETT
NATHANIEL HVIZDOS
JOE METZ
NORMA REDFERN
DEBORAH SNYDER
LARRY TURNER**

ARTWORK CONTRIBUTED BY WORKSHOP MEMBERS

**PHOTOGRAPHS CONTRIBUTED BY
PETER FREDERICK**

THE FREDERICKSBURG CENTER FOR THE CREATIVE ARTS
IS AN AFFILIATE OF
THE VIRGINIA MUSEUM OF FINE ARTS

Copyright © 2005 by The FCCA Poetry Workshop

All rights reserved. No part of this book shall be reproduced or transmitted in any form or by any means, electronic, mechanical, magnetic, photographic including photocopying, recording or by any information storage and retrieval system, without prior written permission of the publisher. No patent liability is assumed with respect to the use of the information contained herein. Although every precaution has been taken in the preparation of this book, the publisher and author assume no responsibility for errors or omissions. Neither is any liability assumed for damages resulting from the use of the information contained herein.

ISBN 0-7414-2435-5

Editing by Susan and Joe Metz

Published by:
INFINITY
PUBLISHING.COM
1094 New DeHaven Street, Suite 100
West Conshohocken, PA 19428-2713
Info@buybooksontheweb.com
www.buybooksontheweb.com
Toll-free (877) BUY BOOK
Local Phone (610) 941-9999
Fax (610) 941-9959

Printed in the United States of America
Printed on Recycled Paper
Published March 2005

TABLE OF CONTENTS

Dedication
   Charlotte Garrett i

"Angels" iii
   Artwork by Cheryl Crane

Prie – Dieu, St. Patrick's 1
   Anne Flythe

Summer And The Leaves Were Green 3
   Charlotte L. Garrett

A Classic Tragedy 5
Pumpkin Halloween 6
Fire 7
   Nathaniel Schellhase Hvizdos

Across the Bridge 8
   Joe Metz

This Afternoon 10
   Deborah S. Snyder

Rain 11
moon-garbed 12
   Larry Turner

Braille 13
Our Need For Magic 14
    Anne Flythe

Soft as a Kiss 15
    Norma Redfern

Song For The Listening Heart 16
    Charlotte L. Garrett

If You And Me 18
Cough 19
    Nathaniel Schellhase Hvizdos

To a Novice at a Country Festival 20
    Joe Metz

"Novice at the Festival" 21
    Artwork by Charlotte Garrett

Fog 22
    Nathaniel Schellhase Hvizdos

Drought Is 23
    Deborah S. Snyder

Spring Thaw 24
    Larry Turner

Werwife 25
    Anne Flythe

"Dogwood Blossoms" 26
   Photograph by Peter Frederick

Catbird Singing in my Dogwood Tree 27
Red Moon Rising 28
   Charlotte L. Garrett

Delicate Joy 29
   Nathaniel Schellhase Hvizdos

Friday Night at the Lodge 31
   Joe Metz

A German Friend 33
   Deborah S. Snyder

Stops on the Way to Eden and Beyond:
The Movie 35
   Larry Turner

Bodies of Water 37
   Anne Flythe

Confession 38
   Charlotte L. Garrett

Wah-Tuh 40
Rain 41
   Nathaniel Schellhase Hvizdos

A Night on the Town 42
   Joe Metz

Lady Leaves Fortune 44
   Deborah S. Snyder

What Dreams May Go 47
   Larry Turner

Moline, Illinois, 1937 48
   Anne Flythe

"Fiorenza" 50
   Photograph by Peter Frederick

Bella Fiorenza 51
   Charlotte L. Garrett

Triple Scoop 52
Is Homeless Hopeless? 53
   Nathaniel Schellhase Hvizdos

My Mother Always Told Me 54
   Norma Redfern

Villanelle To Go 55
   Joe Metz

Pen and ink artwork by
   Nathaniel Schellhase Hvizdos 56

Memory Aid 57
Bodies 58
   Larry Turner

"Invisible" 59
    Artwork by AnneFlythe

Old Women Are Invisible 60
Windfalls 61
    Anne Flythe

Mother's Shoes 63
    Charlotte L. Garrett

Switcharoo 64
Ian Haines 65
    Nathaniel Schellhase Hvizdos

The Trouble with Religion 66
    Joe Metz

This Morning, a Year 69
    Deborah S. Snyder

Scenes from Muckross Friary, Ireland 71, 72
"Passageway", Mellifont Abbey, Ireland 73
"Our Derelict Barn" 74
    Photographs by Peter Frederick

"Appaloosa" 75
"Sandcrab" 76
"Harlequin" 77
"Abuelita" 78
"Eve" 79
"New World Minotaur" 80

"Maize" 81
"St. Francis" 82
"Where Are They?" 83
   Artwork by Anne Flythe

"Country Angel" 84
"To Mr. Satherwaite" 85
"Dear Friend Remembered" 86
"Cherish the Children" 87
   Artwork by Charlotte Garrett

"Faces From a Distant Past" 88, 89, 90, 91
   Artwork by Joe Metz

The Womb 92
   Larry Turner

Hobson's Choice 93
The Other Shoe 94
Shelf Life 95
   Anne Flythe

For Stuart 96
   Charlotte L. Garrett

Top Of The Tree 97
   Nathaniel Schellhase Hvizdos

Somewhere: The Evening Men 99
(Untitled) 102

St. Brigit's Day 103
   Larry Turner

Summer is Running Away 104
   Charlotte L. Garrett

"In Amelia's Garden" 105
   Artwork by Charlotte Garrett

Promise of Spring 106
   Charlotte L. Garrett

How And Why 107
   Nathaniel Schellhase Hvizdos

Melvin Beasley, Veteran 109
   Joe Metz

Truncated Rainbow 111
   Larry Turner

Cutting of the Grass 112
Look to the New Year 113
   Norma Redfern

Bette Davis Lies 114
   Anne Flythe

Living with Ghosts 115
Happiness is not a Place 116
   Charlotte L. Garrett

Effort 117
    Nathaniel Schellhase Hvizdos

Sestina for a Vagabond 119
Old Time Westerns 121
    Joe Metz

One Evening, at Least 122
    Deborah S. Snyder

Year End Prayer 126
    Larry Turner

Ribbet 128
Why Flora Moved To Berkeley 129
    Anne Flythe

Last Night was a Dream 130
    Charlotte L. Garrett

Bathtub Blues 132
    Nathaniel Schellhase Hvizdos

Lamentations From a Fledgling Poet 134
    Joe Metz

The Man Next Door 136
    Larry Turner

Convoys, 1942 138
Ink and Paper 139
    Charlotte L. Garrett

Good People Everywhere 140
Stone 142
   Nathaniel Schellhase Hvizdos

The Second Coming: A Second Opinion 143
   Joe Metz

Ground Zero.. 145
   Larry Turner

They Called Him Crowbar 147
   Nathaniel Schellhase Hvizdos

Judas... 149
My First Sonnets.. 151
   Joe Metz

A Day Without You.. 152
Garden For My Friend 153
Valentine... 154
   Norma Redfern

Talking Head Job... 155
Bitter Half 156
Excerpt From a Pillow Book 157
   Anne Flythe

Twenty Nine Drops Of Oil In The Soup 158
   Nathaniel Schellhase Hvizdos

Symbionts 162
 Anne Flythe

Cats 163
 Joe Metz

Estate of Mind.. 164
Moraine.. 167
 Anne Flythe

Running Away 168
 Charlotte L. Garrett

As 170
Alive?... 172
 Nathaniel Schellhase Hvizdos

Holy Mother... 173
 Charlotte L. Garrett

"Think Godiva Chocolates"................................. 174
 Artwork by Anne Flythe

About the Contributors 175 177

DEDICATION

This first anthology of poetry by members of the Fredericksburg Center For The Creative Arts is dedicated to Cheryl Crane, FCCA President.

The day I first talked to Cheryl about the art world in Fredericksburg and her work, she said, "I paint angels." She does, ably and beautifully, as well as other canvases and drawings that show her inner vision and spiritual inclinations. She serves with true devotion to the arts in this city and its surrounding areas.

There has been renewed enthusiasm from existing members, long-time supporters, various donors, and from the many artists who have been able to exhibit their work in the historic and attractive building that is the Fredericksburg Center For The Creative Arts, 813 Sophia Street.

This anthology of poetry, compiled from the writings of Poetry Workshop members, with paintings, pen and ink drawings, and fine arts photography is, in large part, due to the encouragement and helpful advice given by Cheryl and other members of the Board of Trustees at the Art Center.

Thank you, Cheryl, for your continuing interest and support of our poets and their work.

Charlotte L. Garrett
Chair: Poetry Workshop
FCCA, 813 Sophia Street
Fredericksburg, VA 22410

"ANGELS"

By CHERYL CRANE

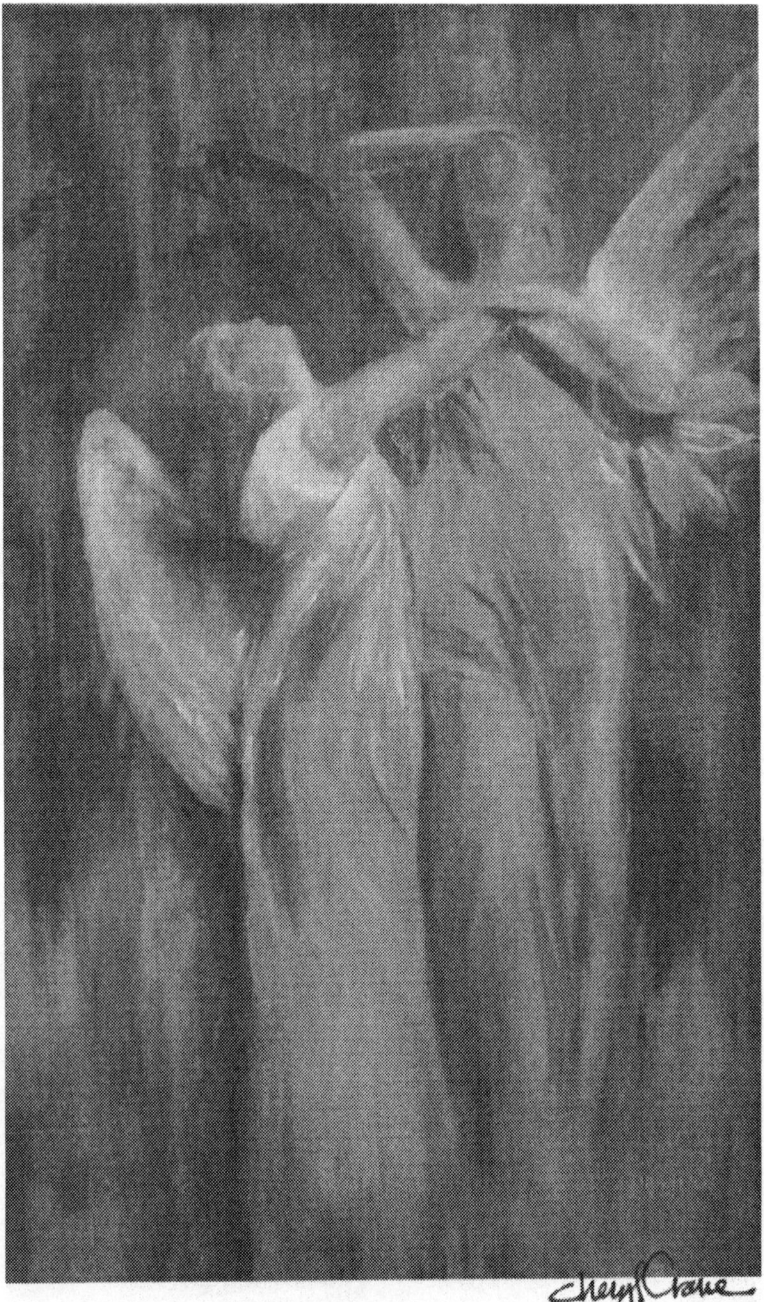
Cheryl Crane

Prie – Dieu, St. Patrick's

◆

Anne Flythe

In still air heavy with the honeyed scent
of beeswax tapers and pale lilies,
within the Gothic sanctity of fluted stone
we sing a mass of supplication,
music so moving it fragments the heart,
lets flow artesian tears.
Milky smoke puffs and spreads from swinging censers,
fragrant for more than two thousand years
of faith and mystery.

A grieving cardinal, splendid in crimson, intones the story
of the almost mythic search
by weeping sweating men to find, to save the living,
to retrieve the dead
if only to separate flesh and bone
from jagged steel and shattered stone.

The gleaming chalice shines
lustrous as an airplane's silver skin.
The sacrament, bone white bread, blood red wine.
We pray those lost were made whole,
that their souls rose skyward
in acrid clouds grown cool
and sweet with myrrh and frankincense.

As we pray for the bereaved,
Father grant us wisdom,
bless our life's work.
It may be

that in our hands we
hold the future,
between our palms
civilization.

Summer And The Leaves Were Green

♦

Charlotte L. Garrett

Summer and the leaves were green,
warm shadows played the lawn
where violets were seen
before their time was gone.
Late day's sunlight searched the grass
to find where roses grew
and when it reached the garden pass
found me waiting there for you.
Waiting and I could not know
if you would see me there
uncertain in my will to go
no longer meant to care
that people passed, their eyes inquiring,
"Why do you wait so long, so lonely?"
Tell them of my quest untiring
to find some season for you only
when we might share in its delights
the joys of time unclocked and free,
forgetful of more worldly plights
than squabbling blue jays in their tree?
Brightened by that bit of dreaming
and the sunset's warming glow,
with the hour's fulfillment
seeming lost, I rose to go.
Then I saw you, joyous moment!
Lips formed words I could not hear.
Gentle man whose kindness God sent,
never mind the fallen tear;

see instead the sudden smile
that curves away from pain
toward laughter that will soar awhile
before returning here again.
Memory loses so much of magic
days and nights that flee
in the semi-comic tragic
patterns of eternity.
So my heart that leaps to yours
unwanted and yet there
holds fast before it pours
words into the summer's air
an image of your smiling lips
that blew to me a kiss
softly from your fingertips,
one your heart can't miss.
To me it was that summer's beauty,
like the sun's soft-lighted flowers,
freeing memory from duty
to recall less pleasant hours.
Will confession bring disfavor
finally when you hear
with how much warmth and love I savor
times when you are near?
In summer, when the leaves are green,
warm shadows play the lawn
where violets are seen
before their time is gone.
Late day's sunlight searches grass
to find where roses grew
and, when it reaches the garden pass,
finds me there with you.

A Classic Tragedy

♦

Nathaniel Schellhase Hvizdos

There once was a lollipop that could talk and like flying birds she could certainly squawk. She would sing and would croon sometimes until noon. Her only good friend was a shriveling balloon. One day in a park while evading a licker, she stumbled to safety in the shade of a pricker. To her surprise she met a thing of her dreams, a big shiny spoon like for scooping ice creams. He greeted her with care and kindness and pleasure. He was intrigued at the sight of this treasure. They talked for hours of this and that when along by the bush strolled a prowling cat. The spoon got defensive and bent out of shape. He flexed his handle and prepared for a scrape. Lolli leaped lightly and prayed for no trouble. Her stick got wobbly and her vision went double. The feline feathered fast and the spoon was aghast. Oh how lucky. Their danger had passed. He straightened his handle and turned with a smile, hoping to resume their talks for a while. His shine dropped to none as if nothing mattered. Luminant Lolli had fainted and shattered. He tingled to a tarnish and lost all ambition, vanquished by Lolli and an eternal love wishin.

Pumpkin Halloween

♦

Nathaniel Schellhase Hvizdos

Out come the demons it's Halloween night
Everyone run in terror and fright
Severed heads and ghosts that scare
It's Halloween night everyone beware
Costumes and make-up hide indentities
Candy for kids saying trick or treat please
Fake blood and real blood blend in the fun
Horror for the masses until the morning sun
Will you stay home or will you go out
Cautiously convene the witching hour's about

Fire

♦

Nathaniel Schellhase Hvizdos

Bursting from the ground
Hot lava builds a mountain
Ebb and flow of earth

Across the Bridge

♦

Joe Metz

On my way to work, across the bridge,
for another day, with thoughts,
only thoughts - - at random - -
when they came, across the bridge,
the other way, for another day
of looking, for another place to stay.
He with crusty brown hair
curled beneath a greasy cap
down onto a ragged shirt.
Few teeth left in the hairy face,
and all his treasures slung in plastic
across a slumping back.
She with the faded coloring of short, tangled hair,
gleaming enough in the sun, starting across the bridge,
to hint of earlier days
when prettiness and promise had come and gone
for more than just another day.
In the seconds of passing, through an open window,
so near, but unaware,
he bent close enough to say some brief something
for only her to hear, for her to share,
coming across the bridge.
And through her wrinkles, the grime,
through the ruddiness of other days in a morning sun,
she laughed.

Looking back, at their mirrored image,
I saw her stroke his arm, moving closer to his side,

while I made my morning turn, across the bridge,
and they were gone.

At the next stop, in the regimented traffic pace
of the morning, in this day,
thinking back, to fix their faces,
the joy of that lingering laugh,
in the face of another day yet to come,
I knew they would be to the other side
of where they had been, where they would go,
before I could return again, across the bridge.

This Afternoon

♦

Deborah S. Snyder

"Porous bones" is
the diagnosis handed to me; and my dreams

are blue brochures of other places,
not here.
Here, the days begin
before sun-up, filled with

traffic. Lucky? You get
your medical, days off, other perks,
I guess. Here is where *vibrant*

refers to the leaves' fall
colors. I set
sticks and bark onto the fire, to
revive it.

Break the stems, first.
Listen. Kindling snaps,
or should: like bones; and then you know it
is useful.

Rain

♦

Larry Turner

Rain.
His rump is planted firmly on the floor.
His pleading eyes look up to me.
He wonders if wagging his tail plaintively
will help his cause.
"No, actually I *would* put out a dog on a night like this."
My foot pushes him out the door onto the deck.
Rain.
I wake from sleep hearing
rainwater rattling along the downspout.
Seldom is there lightning or high wind.
Just rain.
Water stands on the lawn of clay.
The dog's towel scarcely comes
out of the dryer into the cupboard
before it emerges again to dry him..
Rain.
Flowers, grass, shrubs have forgotten the drought,
though river and groundwater remember.
Hard rain drives the dog down two steps
from the deck onto the soggy ground.
Rain.
After a month, some complain—
Enough, already! I still celebrate the rain,
uneasy only about all these animals
gathering two by two.

moon-garbed

♦

Larry Turner

As you sleep the full moon
shining through slats of the blind
dresses you in stripes.
I reach over, grasp your hand,
waiting for the moon to draw us
into enchanted lands.

Braille

♦

Anne Flythe

The wide stone-smoothness of your face
between my hands,
the unexpected softness of straight dark brows
beguile my touch.
The intricate hollow
and swelling of your cheeks,
the shallow bony cups in which
your closed eyes lie
curved faintly moist
as though oiled by tears.
Fine ivory rising beneath
taut flesh forms your
face's cutting edge.
Hard young nostrils flare
with each gentle breath.
How crisply cut your lips
and subtle the transition
from lip to inner mouth
graciously in sleep it curves
young and rich upon your face.
I am content to watch you sleep,
your eyelids such
tender barriers between us.

Our Need For Magic

♦

Anne Flythe

I freed a dragonfly today
spinning wings down in a spider's web
tethered between death and gravity,
a cruciform disaster.
The disentangling was quickly done.
Our need for magic seems still strong,
although I would have intervened in any case.
There seemed a chance of flitterwing's
bright fleeting gratitude –
that my small mercy might earn
some matching grace –
a short reprieve, forgiveness
of a minor trespass or a modest debt.
The spider hungers still,
central to her damaged strategy.
In my gut an iceworm stirs;
whose conjuring have I invoked?
The shallow, pretty spell of glitterwing
or the cold dark glamours
of the fat-bodied one who bides,
who must, and will, recoup her loss?

Soft as a Kiss

♦

Norma Redfern

(Dedicated to Susan Westbrook)

In the dark hours of the night
Death came for me,

Whispering my name,
Soft as a kiss,

Reaching for my hand,
Come with me he said.

Death came for me one night,
Not now I say, another time.

Let me make my peace,
Let me fix what is not finished,

Give me time
To make my peace.

No time is given,
His hand held out for me.

Soft as a kiss he touched my hand,
Come with me.

Song For The Listening Heart

♦

Charlotte L. Garrett

We fight fatigue and the monotony of many miles,
traveling southward, southward,
'til red earth clothes each side of the road
and green grows greener as kudzu castles climb tall as pines.
Warm air, heavy with moisture, hangs like fog,
pressing upon us, upon all we see.
The highway, endless avenue of gray,
is a grim fox-chase, with no winner,
testing both skill and endurance;
but we continue southward, southward.
There is a circled dot on our map that draws us onward;
we know it well.
It lies within the realm of remembered home,
the land long ago left but never forgotten,
the seed bed of our Eden, our beginnings.
Our past, the canvas on which memory paints.
The dot looks small, but once it was the world.
How many times does the car drink gas
while we tilt cans of Coke?
How many dust-dry burgers bulge our belts
as we map check our route?
Sparrows pick in roadside grass
and hornets feast on the trash.
Are all those other travelers seeking the same far haven,
hell bent to get there first?
Pictures of loved ones live in our heads,
too precious to be measured by words;
their faces in us, like bright soft flowers,

glow in both present mind and memory.
They beckon southward, southward.
At last we leave the map,
drive down streets with real houses.
Here are sidewalks and gardens,
the shaded summer paths of playing children.
The roar of the road begins to fade
as softer, sweeter sounds remind us of why we're here;
the South has a music borne on gentle air.
It may twist and torment the heart and wring out tears,
but before the song ends it will comfort,
make balm and solace to cover all the old wounds,
even turn the thin lips of sorrow into a soft smile.
It can do this for those who have ever called it Home.
Its song sings forever to the listening heart.
We're here . . . it has been so long . . .
Time has touched the house kindly.
Fig and pear and Grandmother's roses
frame its corners.
Camellia and dogwood light the lawn.
The screen door opens as we pull into the drive,
and she, the sister, who is the family now,
hurries out to us, her arms open in wide embrace.
We have driven these many miles (I would have walked)
to be thus greeted, to be hugged to the heart,
to be drawn once more into the soft wings of love.
May she always be there when we travel
the long road southward, southward.
She will always be dear to my heart.

If You And Me

♦

Nathaniel Schellhase Hvizdos

Late at night
About to sleep
Thoughts of you
Slowly steep
I am unsure
So I walk timid
You du jour
There is no limit

Cough

♦

Nathaniel Schellhase Hvizdos

Sick with cigarette breath
A step closer to death
Nicotine gets in me
Foggy so I can't see
Tasty tray full of butts
Smoking for sure is nuts
Clearly says you don't care
Secrets that I won't bear
Blood is getting thicker
Feeling somewhat sicker
Just remember
Just remember
Cigarettes will f**k you up

To a Novice at a Country Festival

♦

Joe Metz

So young you gave your life to God. So soon.
Did you decide? Did He? Was there a choice?
You sit on straw, your hands, your feet attune
to fiddle sounds, guitars, a droning drawl
that sings of love and lust you must not feel.
You smile at kids who come to say "Hello"
to God's anointed Child, to see, with zeal,
your face, to touch your shroud of black below
the perfect folds of white atop your hair.
I see a glow of heat adorn your cheek,
as if, down deep, you're suddenly aware
of some deep-seated urge that starts to speak.
I watch you laugh. I think, "She's heard Life call."
But then you genuflect to Brother Paul.

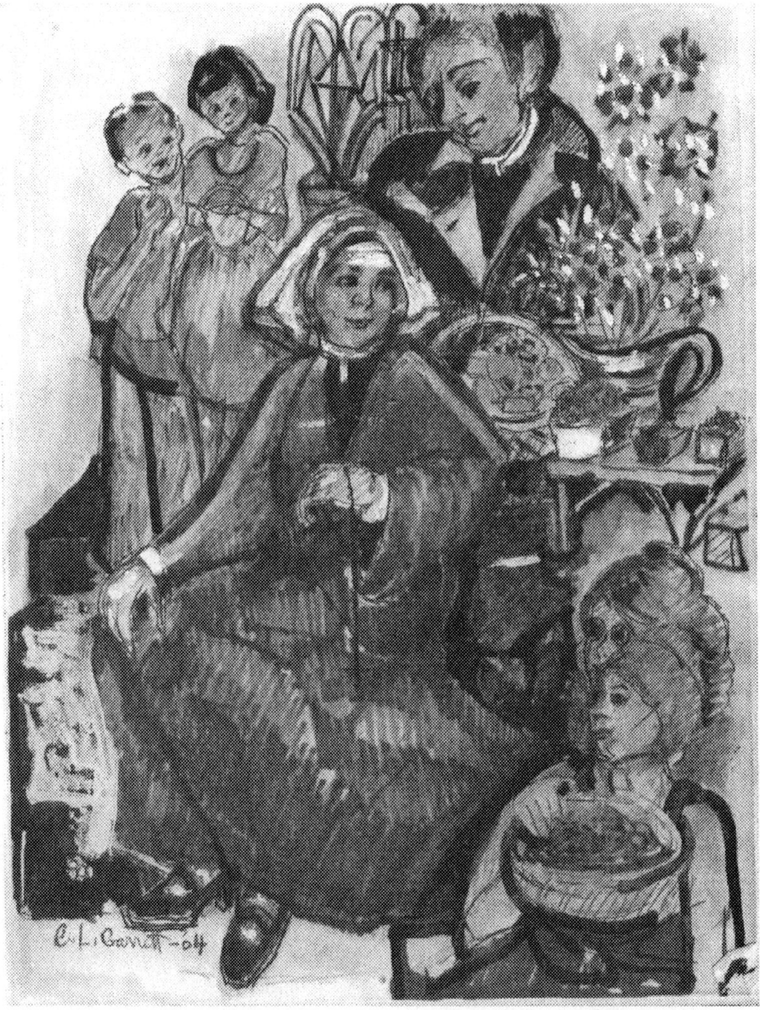

Fog

♦

Nathaniel Schellhase Hvizdos

Fog gently rolls in
Night becomes a misty dream
Illuminated

Drought Is

♦

Deborah S. Snyder

when the sun tarnishes
the raindrops, sending us

scrambling for the brilliant
coins spilling onto the ground.

Chances
of a jackpot, this time?

What riches! Anything we have
it seems, we tamp

into the ground.
And we wait. And as we are waiting, everyone

is looking up. Then the clouds
dissipate. Such

smallness . . . tarapiks, half-shekels . . . when
air this clear

and light, portends
worry. When

bleakness will also,
be bright.

Spring Thaw

♦

Larry Turner

The crocuses blaze in color above the flat and faded grass.
But in Victoria BC the daffodils have been out since February.
    It's time to move on.

The red robin, back from the south, sings his greetings.
But in a Florida park, flamingoes gather by the hundreds.
    It's time to move on.

Grassy lawns are turning green.
But on Dartmoor you see mile after mile of red vegetation.
    It's time to move on.

Trees bud with leaves, and soon forsythia and crabapple will bloom.
But in the California Desert, the joshua tree holds his arms aloft.
    It's time to move on.

With winter chill gone, folks with dogs stroll on the riverwalk.
But in Capri, you can sit in solitude amid rocky cliffs and breaking waves.
    It's time to move on.

Among the faithful, we sing familiar hymns to our risen Lord.
But in Hangzhou, there are festivals to gods I've never even heard of.
Grateful for comfort and friendship, we have stayed too long
in this winter camp, growing fat and prosperous.
Spring is the time of new life, at any age.
    It's time to move on.

Werwife

◆

Anne Flythe

I hunger, shift, and burn:
some part of me no longer deep
beyond day's reach is manifest
in aching jaws, in ivory
that grows and curves within
hot fingertips,
in hair that lifts
and stirs on head and nape until
I, tangled in our bedding, turn
to smell my feral breath
upon your skin and wake
to watch the little pulse
that flutters in your throat.

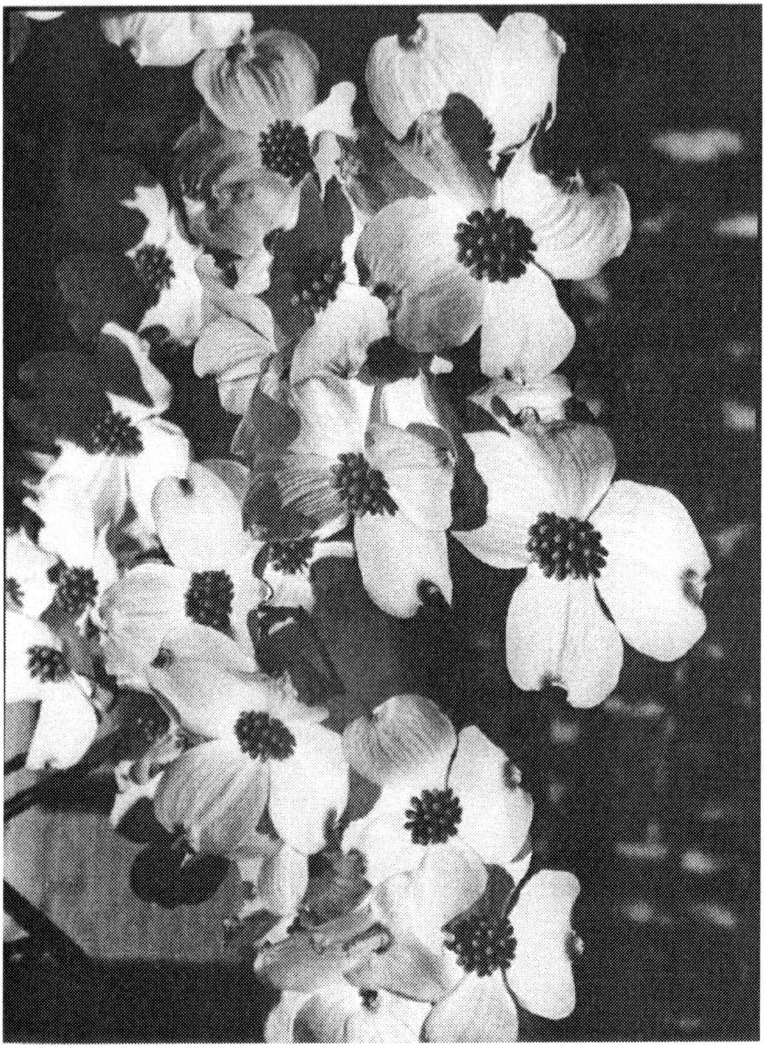

Catbird Singing in my Dogwood Tree

◆

Charlotte L. Garrett

Sparrows crowd the garden,
robins, doves, blue jays too;
but the bird that pleases me
is the catbird singing
in my dogwood tree.
She brings her new family
to feast on grain and seed,
on berries red and purple,
to supply their every need.
I move about on quiet feet,
watching my winged friends eat,
hoping they will stay
near me for awhile
singing their feline roundelay.
Dear little bird, won't you stay
to sing your songs for me?
When winter blows its icy breath,
I will hang seed and suet-bells
upon your tree.

Red Moon Rising

◆

Charlotte L. Garrett

There is a red moon rising
over our faraway hills,
climbing the tops of ink-blue crags
seeking freedom in dark skies.
It is an August moon
on fire in summer air.
Not a whisper of breeze, or spatter of rain,
to lessen dragon's breath heat
here in the palm of the land.
Why do I think of passing time
and the death of happy days?
Has the red moon rising
lighted some old, long-hidden fear?
Days tick by like unwatched hours;
you hair is gray now, and mine.
Yesterday we might have smiled
watching the moon burning,
but now the brevity of our treasured days
uncovers grief, hurling it into the night.
It rises toward darkness with the moon.

Delicate Joy

♦

Nathaniel Schellhase Hvizdos

I once was a shoe that had stepped in poo. I wished to be washed but was tossed instead. I did not go in a can or a bin, but into a lake called Lake Konkamin. I floated for hours 'til the sun did come up. I mingled among leaves, other trash, a foam cup. My day dragged on as I floated along until I ran into a friendly ping pong. I sighed and I frowned. I wanted to be on the ground! Time grew long as the days passed me by. I saw fish and saw birds, they could swim and could fly. I wanted to learn. I wanted to try. I tightened my laces and tucked in my tongue. Life was a ladder, me at the bottom rung. I tried flapping first and then tried to dive. Fish and birds laughed yelling, "What is your jive?" I loosened my laces and took a deep breath. I wanted to drown. I wished now for death. Still I bobbed on until out of the lake. I was in a river now, the river called Snake. There was a reason that it was called that. There were thousands of snakes: long, swimming and fat. I cringed with fear each time they came near. I would shiver and cry yet each time they would swim by. Through bends and curves I kept on going. A river unending it kept on flowing. I met cans and bottles and eventually boats. The boats carried cargo and people and goats. The boats grew in size as the water grew deeper. As the water grew wide I hoped for the Reaper. Through the delta I went and then out to sea. Could this be dreaming, is this really me? I wanted a foot that would hold me and run. Instead I was soaked in salt water and sun. I soon was delirious and then lost my mind. How did I get myself in this terrible bind? My laces curled up and my tongue grew crustaceans. I screamed and I yelled self-righteous degradations. I passed out engulfed at the thought of that poo. Where was I going? What would I do? When I awoke my sole was on sand. I had washed up on a tropical land. Then I looked up the beach and what did I see? A red high heeled shoe who was winking at me!

Friday Night at the Lodge

♦

Joe Metz

They come in,
a little hesitant about where to sit,
about how they'll fit in this Friday night crowd
gathered for the five-piece, rock-a-billy, all-time-favorites,
give-us-your-request band, which is working on
seconds from the bar before it starts to play.

They are up on the floor all at once,
stepping, gliding, twirling with each other,
side-by-side, face-to-face, hand-in-hand,
with the music of memories shared, forgotten, lost,
reaching for a new beat, trying for a new step, listening for a new sound,
on Friday night at the Lodge.

They sit down, with rounds from the bar,
searching for signs that no one noticed
the extra breath, the faltered time, the telling flush,
while the band played on through two-step, rumba, jitterbug, waltz,
and Western lonely lyrics of "hurtin' lost love," too much wine,
of younger years squandered on "them good ol' times."

They move over,
with "Hello's" to new Brothers, with nothing from the bar,
just now coming to hear enough of this Friday night's sounds
to relieve long days, occasional calls, odd jobs,

fixed income, monthly check-ups, mall walking, TV specials,
and dinner for two, only where it's all-you-can-eat.

They go out another time onto the floor, as the band,
fresh from break and another pass by the bar, loosens up the volume,
with a new beat, a new sound, of hard driving rock, for a change, man,
blasting it out on the system, getting it on loud, stringing it out with flashing hands,
while the Brothers boogie it out for a bit, then, all but one couple, searching for a new step,
return to sit silent at their tables until this piece, this time, is over.

They go to the stage,
this last couple on the floor, lost in their new step, pounded by the beat,
asking the band to take their next piece from another time, before their time,
when there were softer sounds, slower beats, maybe better times,
a piece everyone here can remember, can dance to, have fun with,
because, on this time of week, that's what we come here to do.

They go back to their table,
smiling now, listening to the system sending out a waltz tune,
which brings everyone to the floor again, knowing that it's fine now,
that the right beat, the right time, the right step, has come back again,
because the band knows now that face-to-face, side-by-side, hand-in-hand,
the Brothers need the music of memories on Friday night at the Lodge.

A German Friend
(SPRINGFIELD, MA, USA - 1961)
♦
Deborah S. Snyder

"The world had merely begun to learn in detail what happened . . . . "
(a paraphrase).
---- Encyclopedia of the Holocaust, on the trial of Adolf Eichmann, 1961

The sky barely fit, a lid
stretched
over the blue stream, and the knoll

where we stopped, out of breath
sprocket and gear, pine
needles and grass blades

poking us. I could never keep up, always seeing
Gretchen's platted hair bright
tassels flying. Dinnertime,

and night like coal filling a bin,
her mother calling her home, smiling
as we walked in.

Inside, a fire, Gretchen's father walking
from it, to table. Always, it seemed, a yellow broth
with Saltines, and the *Spatzle*: wide noodles

like in a lukshen kugel, *Klops* and these
almond crescents, and milk for us.
No one minded me being there, I'd think

how nice they all were, and this – the same year
I began to keep noticing
her brothers:

like planking, and my turning
away. *And evening
becomes night.*

Stops on the Way to Eden and Beyond: The Movie

◆

Larry Turner

See, it hasn't been done, making a movie
from a book of poems. Well yes, *Old Possum's
Book of Practical Cats* did give us that musical.
And yes, there are some problems, continuity and such.
Still—

      Already I'm scouting out locations:
The cave where Lot and his daughters settled.
Road from Anacapri down to the Blue Grotto.
Field of purple bluebells.
Thick-walled jail in Lilith.

You think I'm egotistical, making a poem
about making a movie out of my own poems?
What about Yeats and his circus animals?
(Not much of an accomplishment,
being no more egotistical than Yeats.)

The nice thing about casting is, I'm not
constrained by money or time. I can put
Humphrey Bogart and Julia Roberts in the same scene
and make them each any age I like.
For narrator, I'm thinking of Tom Cruise,
but I'll probably settle for Woody Allen.

Maybe you can help. Who should do
Eve of Earth, Eve of Life, Adam,
Sophia, the Chief Ruler,
the banker's wife, the commuter,
the traveler, the gentle butcher,
the piano student and her teachers,
Laurie and her lovers, Heidi and her father,
Owain and the princess,
the girl who offered me wings?

Some things here you don't recognize?
Wait for the movie.
Or buy the book.

Bodies of Water

♦

Anne Flythe

The siphon is working,
one and a half inch PVC,
a smooth black conduit
from lake to empty pond.
Cool clear water
pulses from the pipe,
an umbilical connection thrumming
with the bright power of water.
This morning William called.
Rebecca's water broke
too soon.
The small internal lake
gushed warm and cloudy,
the stranded fingerling
no longer gilled, but unprepared
for this dry world.

Confession

♦

Charlotte L. Garrett

Taking the narrow path that points to where you are;
slowing as I reach the gate seeing how near the door,

longing to be inside but dreading the moment before
I pause to look around the yard where trees and grounds are gray

and all that moves and all that breathes
is a girl who turns away

as though to leave and not return
to see this solemn place.

I would have left but for the thought of your kind and smiling face.
Three steps more, I reach the door and opening stand quite still.

The sounds of life are stronger here; they brace my weakening will.
Then you are there; we smile "Hello."

Happy now I have no wish to go.
We speak of time that has gone by, of things we think and do,

of books we read, of work well done, of dreams for the future too.

I watch your face. It pleases me to see you there

wearing the look of wise content, tracings of silver in your hair.
The dark of your suit is comforting to me; it bids me to confide

those thoughts so often hidden away that others may not know
who chide us for our foolishness and seek to change us. No.

My tears are falling, warm and free; how grand it is to cry.
I had not dreamed of doing so, yet what release it brings.

I know that nowhere have my tears been understood so well
or that having let them fall

I could be so glad they fell.
It's time to go. I rise and then it seems so hard to do,

to leave the place where I have talked in secrecy with you.
I shall come back and bring a much more happy heart.

Perhaps it will be Spring by then and be less sad to part.
The narrow path will lead the way:

I shall have left my heart.

Wah-Tuh

♦

Nathaniel Schellhase Hvizdos

Water
Water
The opposite of fire
Water is essential for our survival
If you control the water then you are a sire
Do not be dismayed if you pay for it too
Looking around most of us do
Turn towards oceans and rivers and streams
Oh how it's gushing beauty beams
Sparkling sunlight
It takes many people to harness it
Water so cool in a glass from the tap
I think I will have a glass before I nap

Rain

♦

Nathaniel Schellhase Hvizdos

Ancient grass still grows
In its fashion seeds are born and reborn
We remember all until we forget
Soil nourishes
Rain is food
Each blade cut
Each blade dies only to return back to the Earth
To Sun
To solar system
Universe
See struggle
Rain eternal nourishment
Until now pollution pours down on us
Feel us perishing each drop
Lost from form
Found
Kiss the ground
Seek less
Give more
Lead the masses
A cry
Help
Unheard our children will cry

A Night on the Town

◆

Joe Metz

Late shift, around midnight, or so,
when these two come in,
go take the booth by the window.

She's dyed blonde, around forty, or so,
stretch jeans and boots,
from someplace expensive uptown.

He's cute, around twenty, or so,
khakis and loafers,
maybe a college kid from across town.

"Hi folks. What can I get you?"
And he says: coffee.
and: uh, some for her too.
"Need cream and sugar?"
And he says: yeah, little cream in both,
and: how about some pie, you got chocolate?
"Yeah, there's a piece or two over there."
And he says: O.K., I'll get a piece.
and: I guess her too.
"Anything else tonight?"
And he says: nope, that's it.

So, I bring their coffee, with a little cream,
with the pie, with the check.
And he says: thanks.
and: let her have it, she's paying it all tonight.

"Well, that's real nice of her."
And she says: (nothing)

He wolfs down the pie, swallows his coffee,
still steaming enough to make sweat,
lights up a cigarette from a pack
she'd put on the table when they first came in.
And he says: you ready to go?
And she says: (nothing)

He walks for the door first,
while she gives me cash, with a tip,
while I'm seeing the coffee she never touched,
the pie she didn't eat and, as she heads out,
the tears she's trying hard to hide.

"Thanks for coming in.
"Hope you both have a real good night."
And he says: yeah, sure.
and: hey, hurry up will you!
We still got a little time left.
And she says: (nothing)

I clean their table, clear the register,
put out the lights, and think of her
going out the door,
wondering if all
she'd ever found
out there was
nothing, or so.

Lady Leaves Fortune

♦

Deborah S. Snyder

Call it what you will. But first,
look up. What do you see

or hear? Listen.
Beyond the clearing: the pines
are whistling.

And the apple, through
the boughs; and the weeping willow, its
hair scraping

alongside the house. Against the siding,
screeching: so

that chalk comes to mind.
Merely the *noise*
of wind, and I find: enough to chill

the Earth, now. Starlings fly out
of the warm vents, building in them.
Comes a knocking on my door,

greetings. Mind
if we stay, awhile?

Everyone visits me wanting my house, overstays
his or her welcome, leaves
but only after half the night has passed.

Starry night – overhead, is in shards.
And yet
it isn't.

I am seeing the leafless branches
which ways poke the stars,

and only lend the effect: everything
actually will grow again, and soon. First
it snows, and yet the storms

are quilts placed over every
living thing, as it sleeps. See that
sparrow, settling in?

Snowflakes kiss
the berries and cones, as the bird searches.
Neither wing nor beak – nothing

is slowing down in the squall, snow
has not missed the giant oak
on its side,

that lightning once struck, that
which was a feast

for the termites and carpenter ants forgotten
by even them, now.
Snow falls onto it, curiously. So I note: snow

regards everything which exists. Far fetched,
I guess, yet, who can say? Who
so loved the world, is

to then judge all of it,
right?

My cat
springs onto my lap circling
or wanting to, purring as I read.

She naps. This for me, completes
the picture: bay window of beveled glass,
beyond which

the corn snow has
slid from the budding branches . . .
the *kindness*

in that image . . . O.
Oh, I have lawyers. Sisters, brothers; nieces,
nephews, and the

gall of all of them
to send these emails; the notarized
scratches they call *signatures;*

and the commitment papers.
Kindness
toward me years ago, informed

my decision, bringing me
peace if you will, giving scope to my reasons:
rationale. Of sound mind

means, capable of reason, does it not?
Precisely: and which is just
as the Courts just found.

What Dreams May Go

◆

Larry Turner

Suppose
when you wake, the dream goes on.
The flight you feared to miss takes off
with someone from standby in your seat.
The car you couldn't find sits there
a few days, then is towed to the impound lot.

But you don't care.
You've left that world of unreality
and people who suddenly change
their age and identity.
You're awake.

Now suppose
when you die, it's not like falling asleep
but like waking from a dream.
The concerns that dogged your working days,
the worries that kept you awake nights,
even the brooding over your family
and their problems,
all resolve themselves
without you.

You've left that world of injustice
and people who age slowly
and change their minds fast.
Your attention turns
from what you're awaking from
to what you're awaking to.

Moline, Illinois, 1937

♦

Anne Flythe

Fireflies' small green glows rose
and fell in air as thick as simple syrup.
Across the yards the cries and laughter
of children playing after-supper games
were muted as women standing in their kitchen doorways
called them home before a coming storm.
Hyacinthine lightning fragmented
the mazarine horizon's classic curve.
Paranoid as Chicken Little,
a flight of lapis jays
jeered wildly in the storm light,
flashing over beds of iris
rambunctious as puppies,
jarring petals from the pear trees.
As distant thunder muttered counter threat,
a rising wet wind set the great elm
trees to thrashing in the liquid light.
Electrified, the frantic guardians
of summer's status quo
renewed their jangling alarms.
Panicked jays fled before the wind,
only to fall silent, failed, beneath
the savage onslaught of rain
that emptied yards and porches,
drove day's last light indoors.
By nightfall the intoxicating fragrance
of summer rain on fresh-cut grass arose
to mingle with the stony scent of

wet pavement, sidewalks, roads.
There was no conflict in the mild, sweet smoke of pipe
tobacco, as the murmuring of adult voices recommenced.
Summer sounds - the creak of swings and wicker rocking
chairs,
punctuated by the twang and slap of screen doors closing,
the silvery clink of iced-tea spoons in tall glasses - -
on long wide porches that wrapped life safely against
our houses then, only to become again domestic stages
where actors resumed their classic roles before
audiences long familiar with all the plays.
An insistent mourning dove, soft-voiced and wakeful,
warned that what had come and gone so violently would
come again: storms inevitable as death; war, winter
or the return of summer, and when summer came again
children played now long-forgotten games as always.
After supper, in the gathering blue dusk, their distant
shouts and laughter in synchrony with heat lightning
flickering at the edge of vision.

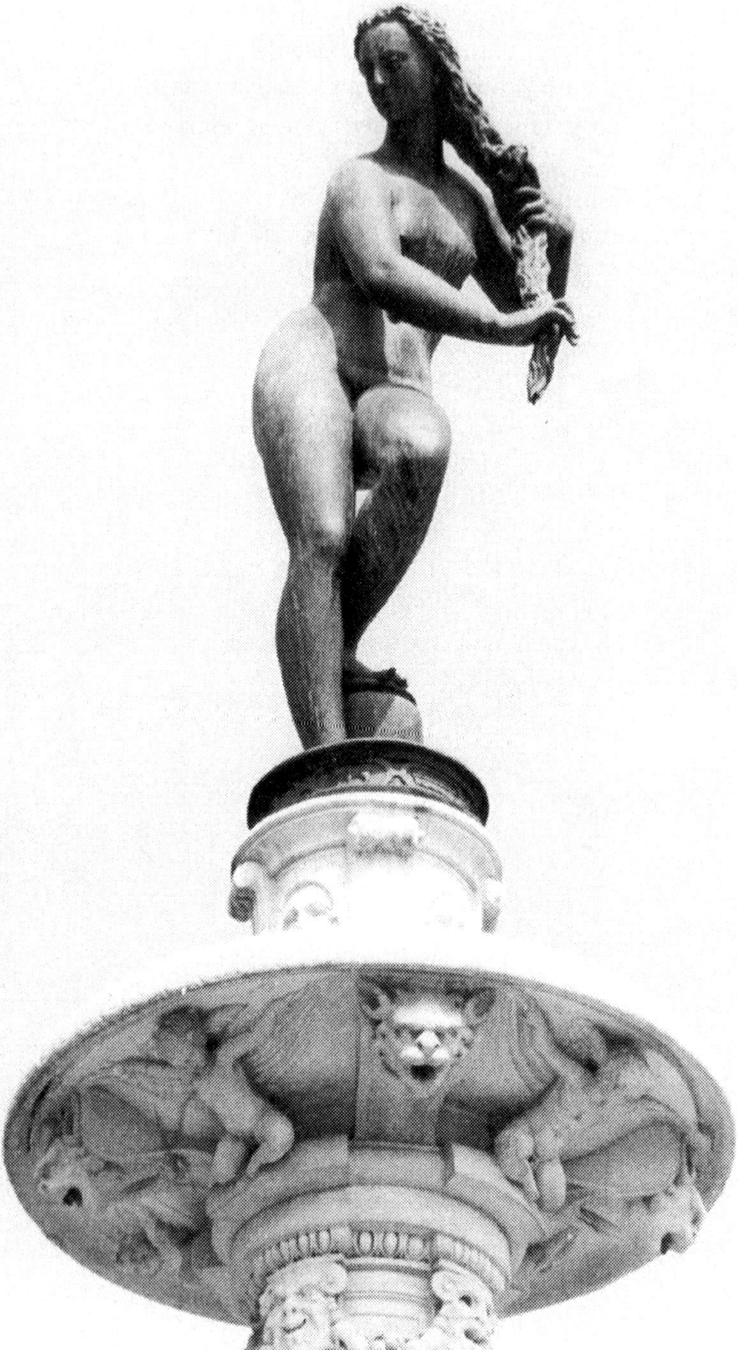

Bella Fiorenza

♦

Charlotte L. Garrett

Dancing girl, let down your hair.
Admiring eyes clearly stare at your loveliness.
May your partner soon confess his everlasting fascination,
and if you wish it, we, our admiration . . .
it shall be given.
Grant you his everlasting love;
let no envious eyes deter him from his passion's quest.
You alone shall please him best.
Give love truly.
Be seldom unruly.
Never deceive him.
Bella Fiorenza, do not leave him bereft and in despair;
let down your hair.
Together dance, take his hand: later wear his wedding band.
Hear the music, let it play, let it warm your heart today.
Allow his hand to touch your hair.
Your pretty hands and dancing feet are feathers in the air.
Hear his words in you ear; they can banish foolish fear.
Let his kisses dry your fallen tears –
he loves you now as he has for years.
Let your partner circle you with his arms.
Trust his strength to banish harms.
Let your heart be free from fear.
Your beloved is always near.
Help his eyes to remain as bright as they are this very night.
May your joy last forever, dancing girl.

*Based on a photograph on the previous page by Peter Frederick, "Fiorenza", a statue in Florence, Italy

Triple Scoop

♦

Nathaniel Schellhase Hvizdos

Miss Mary Mack
Was smoking crack
She coughed up black
And lunched on sack
Her breaths grew short
She needed snort
Or little pills
To cure her ills
The nights grew long
The days were longer longer
Until she fell
Right on her face
A sad disgrace
She sold her mace
And then her twat
Her head grew hot hot
She reached the top
And she plunged off to her concrete plot

Is Homeless Hopeless?

♦

Nathaniel Schellhase Hvizdos

I find no time for standing in line
And only white when I look for red wine
So I cashed my check and gave it all away
Living from trashcans to this very day

My Mother Always Told Me

♦

Norma Redfern

Pick up after yourself
Put it away when you are finished
Always make your bed when you get up
Put your clothes away
Fix breakfast, clean up after
Your kitchen will always be neat and clean
Never go to bed with dishes in the sink.

Teach your children
good habits and you will be rewarded
Pick up quickly before you go to bed
When unexpected company
says they will be stopping by
the house will always be in order.
These are the things

my Mother told me all my life.
Alas, alas I say,
I never did the things she told me to do
unless she was standing right over me.
The older I get and look back on my life
how I wish I would have listened,
then my house would not be such a mess.

Villanelle To Go

♦

Joe Metz

Pizza Hut and Chick-Fil-A,
Main Street Deli and Burger King - -
I go for fast food every day.

They say it's made just my way - -
their crispy crust and chicken wing - -
at Pizza Hut and Chick-Fil-A.

Though lots of salt comes into play,
too few onions, not much zing,
I go for fast food every day.

"Their fat's not good", experts say.
"You're blocking some aortic ring
at Pizza Hut and Chick-Fil-A."

That could be true in every way,
but I can't help but do my thing
and go for fast food every day.

Make subs and burgers "all-MY-way,"
set out a feast at Burger King,
at Pizza Hut or Chick-Fil-A - -
I love my fast food every day.

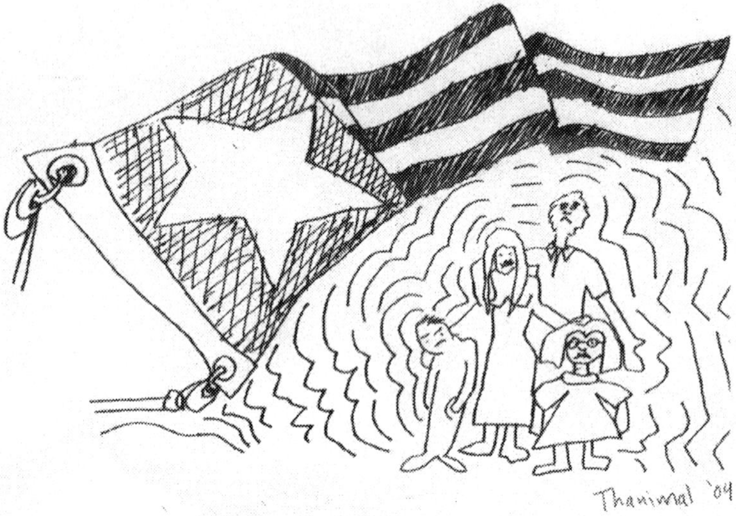
Thanimal '04

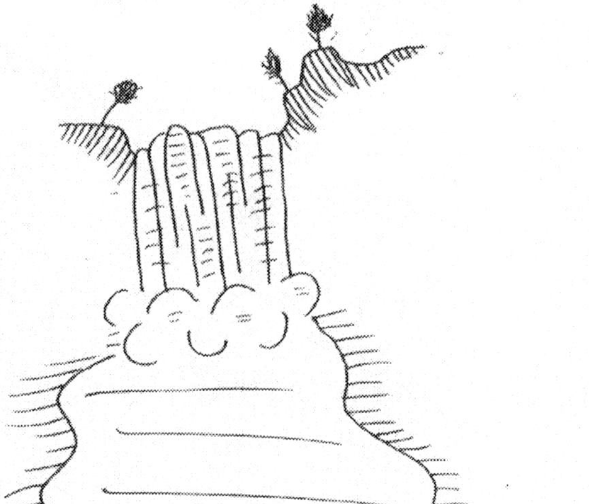
Thanimal '04

Memory Aid

♦

Larry Turner

I don't need
Flags on my car and lapel
Uncle Sams on my lawn
Eagles on my walls
Red, white and blue ornaments
on my Christmas tree.
Even without these
I remember
I love my country.

Bodies

♦

Larry Turner

We are trying to sort out the bodies
of our soldiers from their soldiers.
But why bother? Why not just
bury them here together.

After all,
they were all young
and Died for Their Country
in a war they thought right
or at least necessary
or at least personally unavoidable.

After all,
there is less difference among them
than between them
and those on both sides
who sent them here.

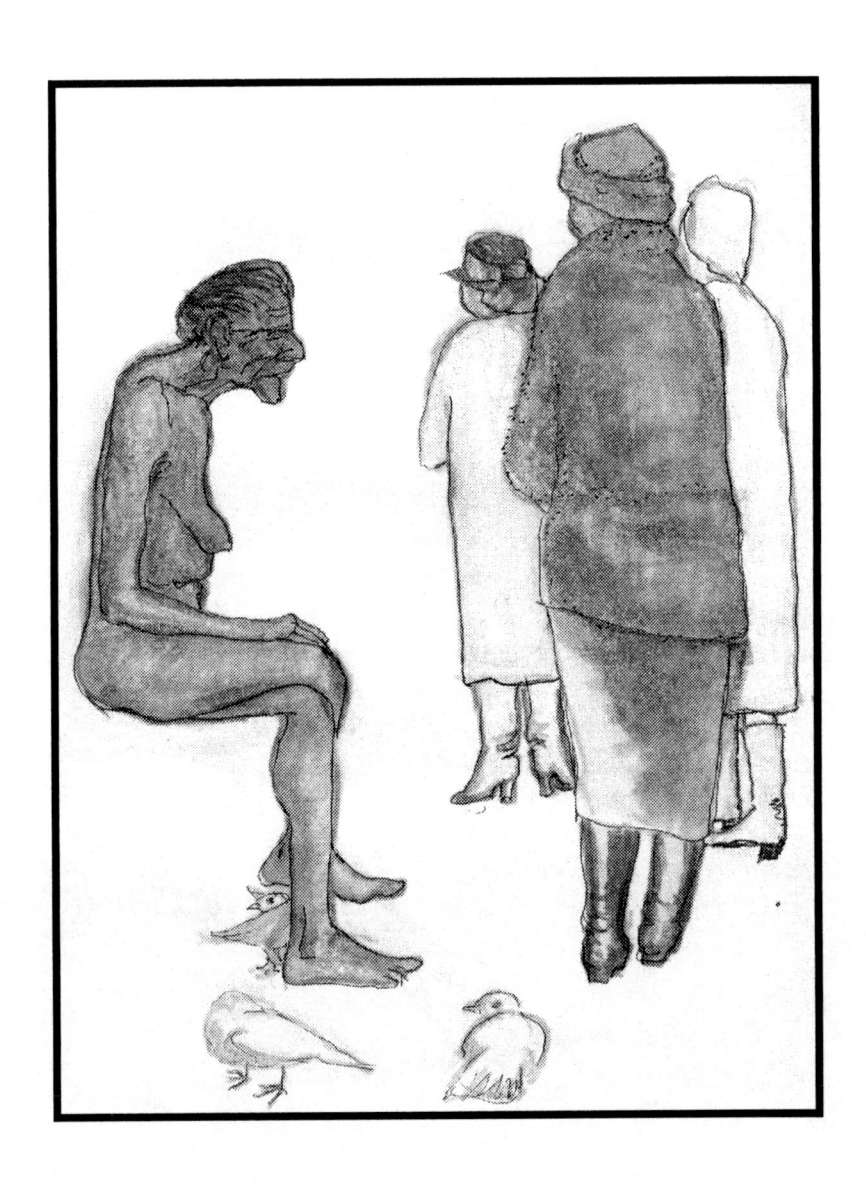

Old Women Are Invisible

♦

Anne Flythe

Hipshot, shirtless, he stood
in the small dark post office,
both hands filled with mail.
Late day sun slanted through the open doors
gilding the strong curve of his naked back,
young skin moist and shining,
brown forearms lightly thatched with golden hair.
The sudden chiaroscuro made her heart lurch.
Her belly tightened at her hands' sure knowledge
of how they would change their shape
to trace that long smooth line.
A dizzying awareness of this scent,
stronger than the faint janitorial pine,
caused her breath to catch,
a heartbeat away from touch.
What would he have thought, said, done,
at such presumption?

Windfalls

♦

Anne Flythe

The woods are close, dark and wild,
encroaching on the limited neutrality
of our rough lawn and garden,
too ordered to invite familiarity,
not tamed enough for pride.

A fine dry snow is falling,
an inch or more lies on the smoking ground,
already boundaries are lost in sifting white.
As suddenly as by sleight of hand, a vixen
stands beneath our wild persimmon tree,
insubstantial in the milky light
except for sable mask, tail tip,
and penpoint feet that stipple prints
among the thickly scattered fruit.
Jaws scissoring with dainty greed she feasts.
At intervals, she lifts and turns
her lovely feral head to cup
the smallest change in silence.
Licking sticky chops with narrow tongue,
testing the air as though she tastes
a sound I cannot hear.
Shadowless, she drifts away like smoke.
The yard is curiously luminous and flat.
The fox's markings black as brush strokes
on watercolor paper.
She shrinks into this
singular dimension,

dwindling to distant
punctuation marks
on smooth white
emptiness.

I wish the woods
lay farther from the house,
or that there was
less wilderness in me.

Mother's Shoes

♦

Charlotte L. Garrett

Mother's shoes were black, with laces,
sturdy heels and well-buffed shine.
They may have walked a thousand miles.
"Sturdy," you said, "to last
like me and mine."
You said you knew my heart was full;
we laughed and cried together . . .
that was the bond we shared.
Few words were ever needed;
I knew you cared.
Are you still with me? Yes.
Your voice echoes when I hear my own.
Your smile, your eyes and hair
glow warmly alive in your portrait
on the living room wall.
You are there as I enter the hall.
Did you know how much you were loved
by my children, husband, my brother, sister, and me . . .
by father and so many more . . .
even by shoppers in your store?
My friends admire the picture I painted
before saying goodbye at the door.
They see how proud of you I've always been.
Tonight I remember your shoes;
tomorrow another memory I may choose:
a dress, a coat, or one of the many
hats you wore.

Switcharoo

♦

Nathaniel Schellhase Hvizdos

Fields full of cows waiting to die
Lunking big mass with pain its eye
Pushing against barbed wire into its head
Bumbling beasts who seek grass till they are dead
They fill up the pastures fields full side by side
Killed parceled packaged flank rump and hide
They are raised just like chickens to feed human masses
We even eat hot dogs which include parts of asses
Others eat feet of chicken and hogs
Still more eat legs of lamb and of frogs
Incisors and canines for ripping flesh
Molars for veggies and fruits that are fresh
An age of infection could cause it to still
Or a conscious decision using your will
I used to be a vegetarian like some people you know
It is something to ponder as you age change and grow

Ian Haines

♦

Nathaniel Schellhase Hvizdos

Rocks wood earth
All our friends
Clocks could not work for all our friends
The quiet ones in a loud group scene
Often I wonder what does it mean
I know sometimes I don't talk when I think
Others I speak and don't think when I drink
What do they ponder and where are their goals
What do they do to fill time's dragging holes
With hands in their pockets and eyes on the floor
Hoping no one thinks me bored lonely or sore
Time tick tocks past me as I drink it away
Waiting in pain for my weekend payday
With dinero upon me its time I must shout
Relinquishing all I stray and get out

The Trouble with Religion

♦

Joe Metz

Well, I think the trouble with religion
is knowing which one is and which one isn't
the pathway to the Promised Land,
with some Holy Host, hand-in-hand.

When I thought I'd be an Episcopalian,
my friends all said, "You'll seem so alien!"
So I looked into the Anabaptists,
a faith in which Love enwraps us.

But being Amish or a Mennonite
just didn't leave me feeling right,
so I read Ron Hubbard's "Scientology,"
hoping to fathom his new theology.

Still, "Dianetics" and a state of "Clear"
just weren't that pleasing to my ear.
I said, "I quit!" - - without being hostile,
and pondered becoming a Pentecostal.

Speaking in tongues, faith as healing,
swept me right up in a spiritual feeling
that was all too easy to see the Truth in,
I sought a new challenge -- being a Lutheran.

There I became both saint and sinner,
a loser in my eyes, in God's eyes a winner.
I studied the Bible, reviewed every sermon,
wishing I'd learned lots more about German.

Yet all of a sudden, with Salvation ahead,
a new urge for learning popped into my head.
Though friends said, concerned, "Don't try to elude us!"
Nirvana in mind, I declared, "I'm a Buddhist!"

I guess some might say I rushed in too quickly;
my orange robe was scratchy, my head glistened slickly.
Still not enlightened, though I studied the *dharma,*
I knew begging for alms was not part of my *karma!*

Now I was worried - - "How many more choices?" - -
when my good Catholic friends lifted their voices,
inviting me to seek revelation and hope,
by looking toward Rome, the power of the Pope.

I studied about apostolic succession,
attended each Mass, vented sins at confession.
Still there was this thought, while I was fasting,
that my time as a Catholic might not be lasting.

That proved to be true, so like a risk taker,
I devoted myself to becoming a Quaker.
Plain clothing, plain language, virtues to see,
with love for all people, especially Thee.

I practiced my faith, against death, against war,
continuing to wonder if I'd find something more,
some other salvation for the hopeless and hapless,
like being a Mormon or a good Southern Baptist.

Could I pray like a Muslim? a Hindu? a Jew?
I shouted with anguish, "What can I do?"
My friends all replied, "Just come to *my* church!"
thus leaving me in a liturgical lurch.

My problem is solved now, at least for a while.
I think I've selected a system with style.
Each day I read analects of moral profusion
and study Chinese as a fledging Confucian.

This Morning, a Year

♦

Deborah S. Snyder

begins, and sparrows
drift, an ash fall

settling among the treetops'
newest stems.

Daybreak puts out the morning
star's wick, sputtering

as whitecaps are flailing
now thinly

slipping from view. How youthful
leaving, really is. Sails leaning

into everything: wind, chances, skies
which are chafed, now

redly warning
rain is approaching

so quickly, there is no time.
Land, of

stillness. The rock face
of naval vessels jutting

from the surface and taking most of a day
to reach the horizon – an advance

which only seems slow, moving glacially, actually
is an illusion. Taking place, is nothing

is about to ever be
the same again.

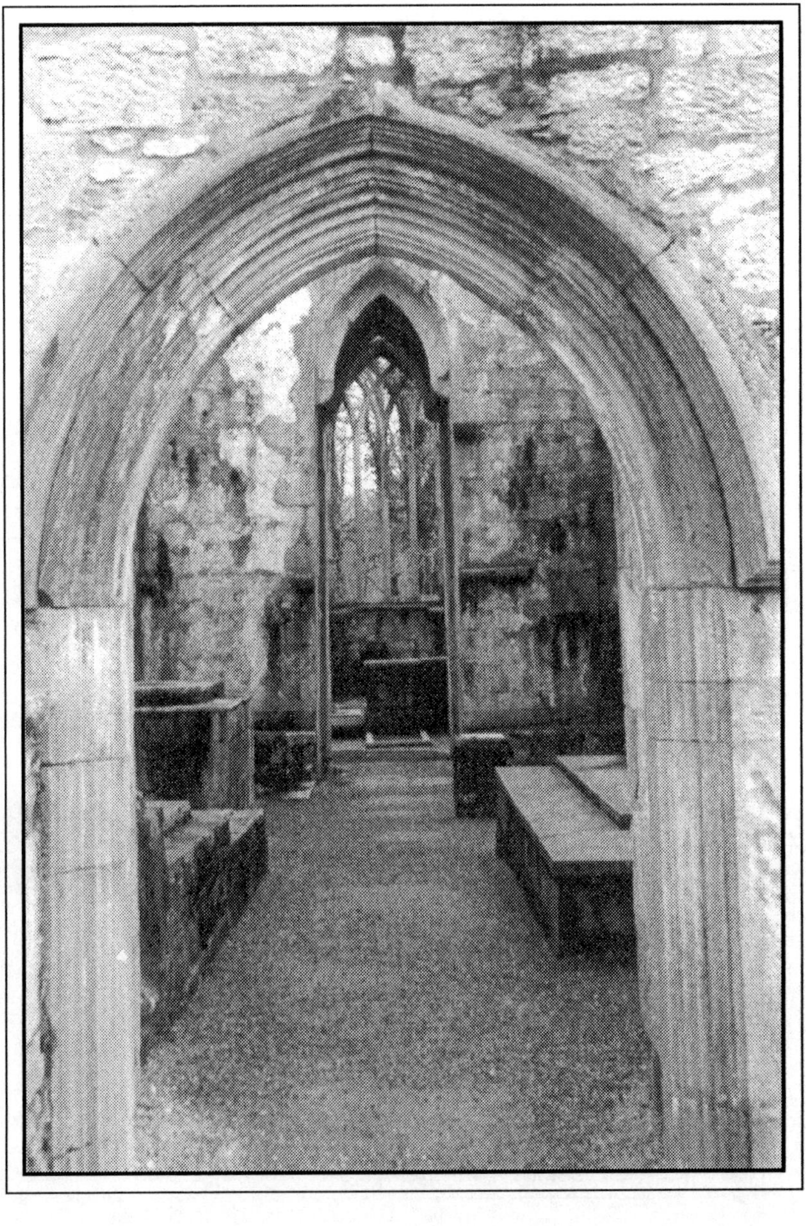

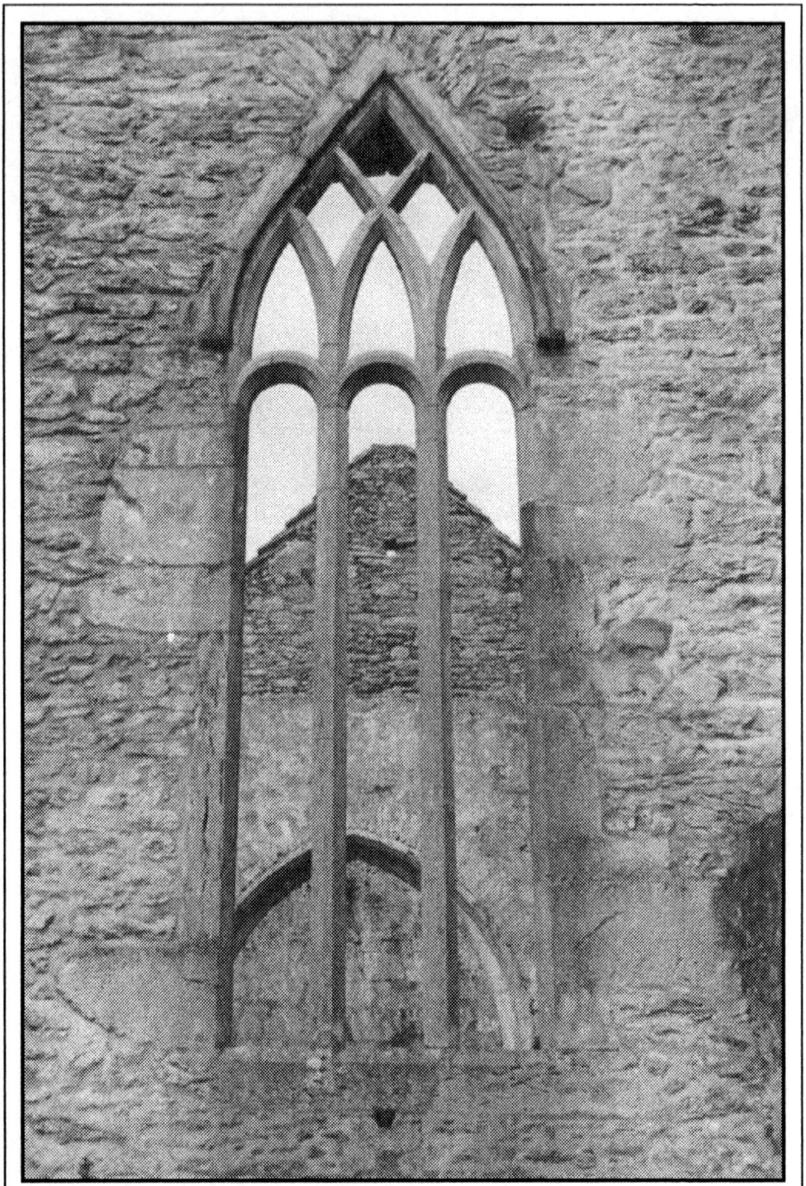

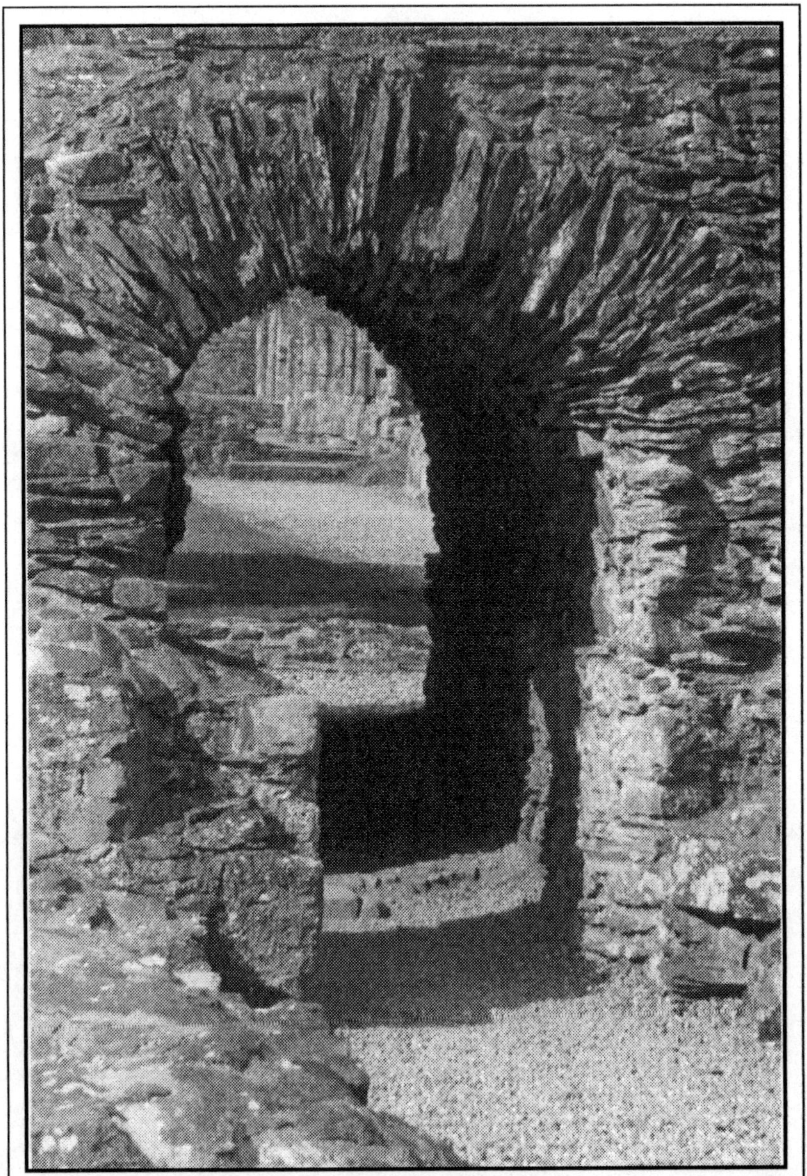

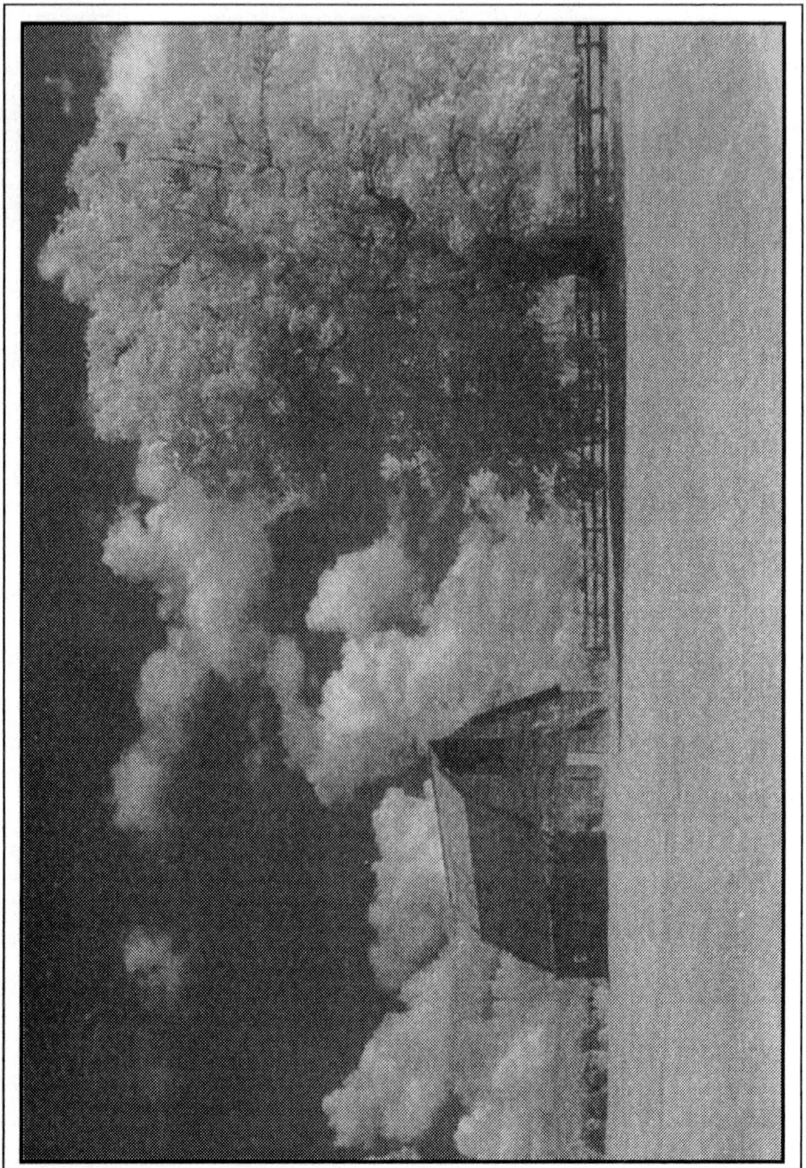

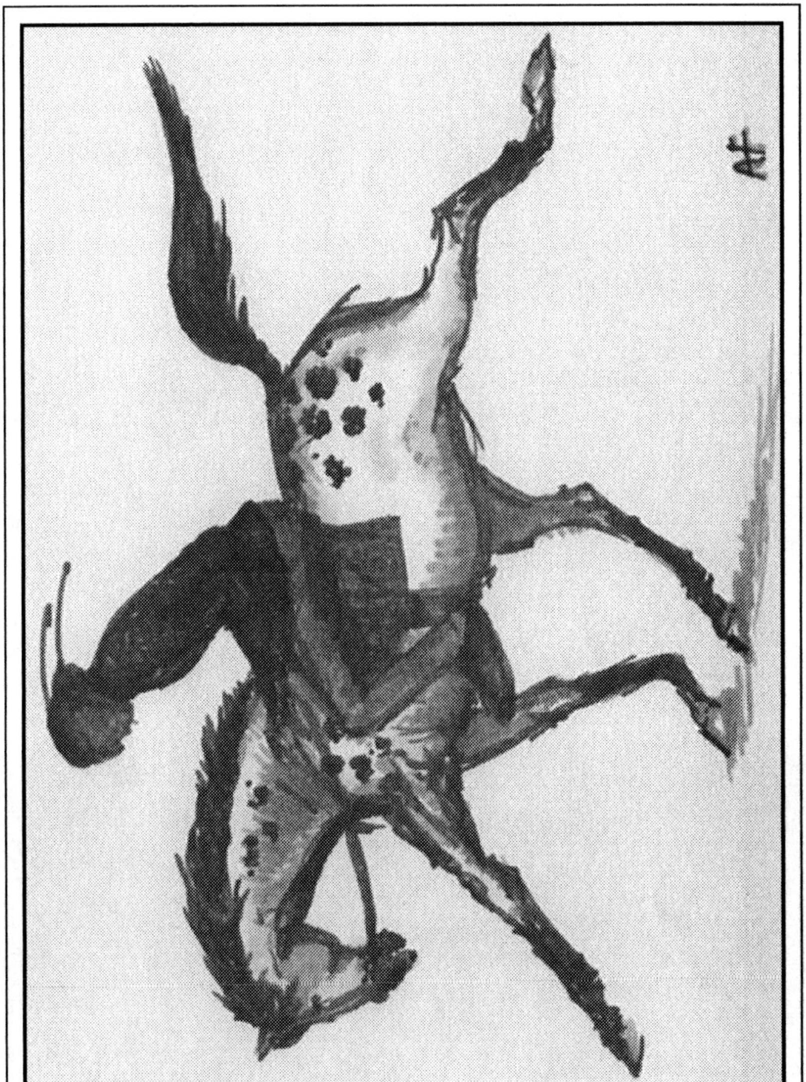

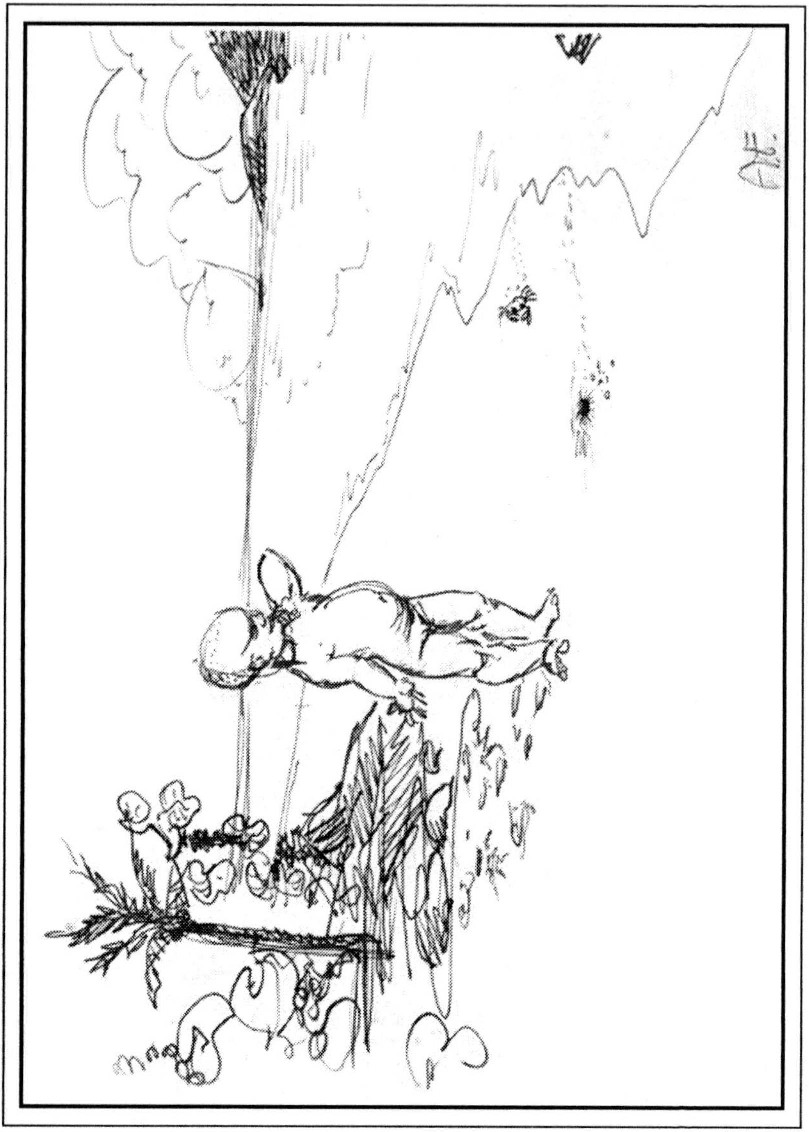

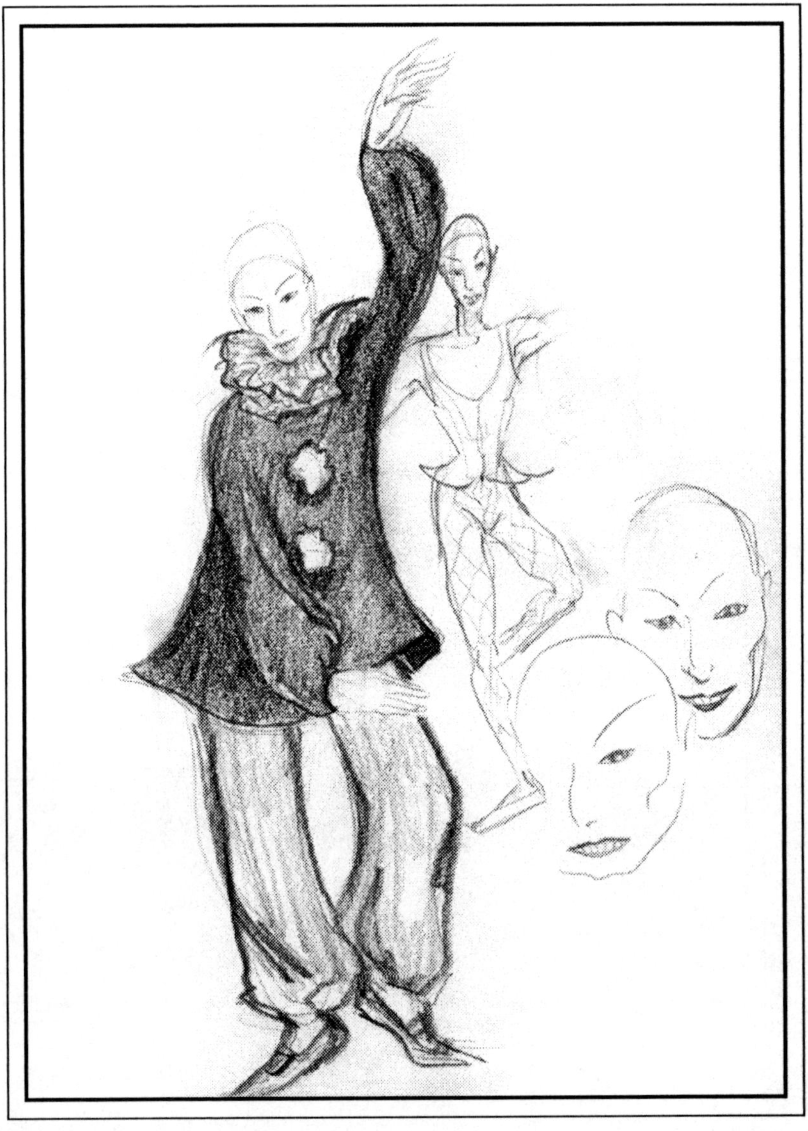

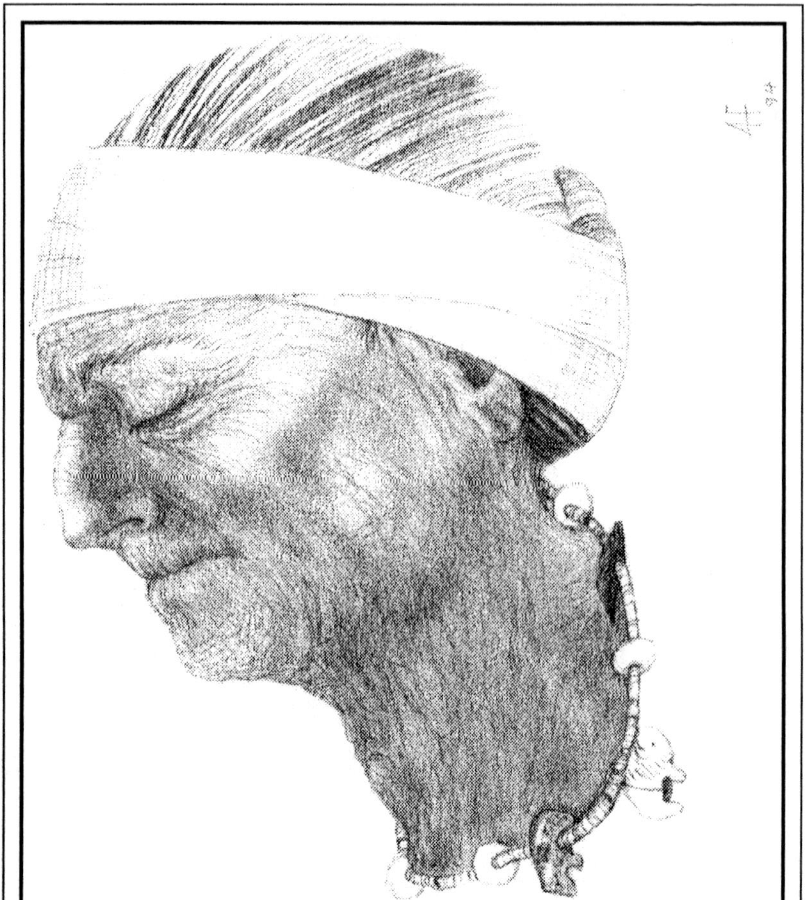

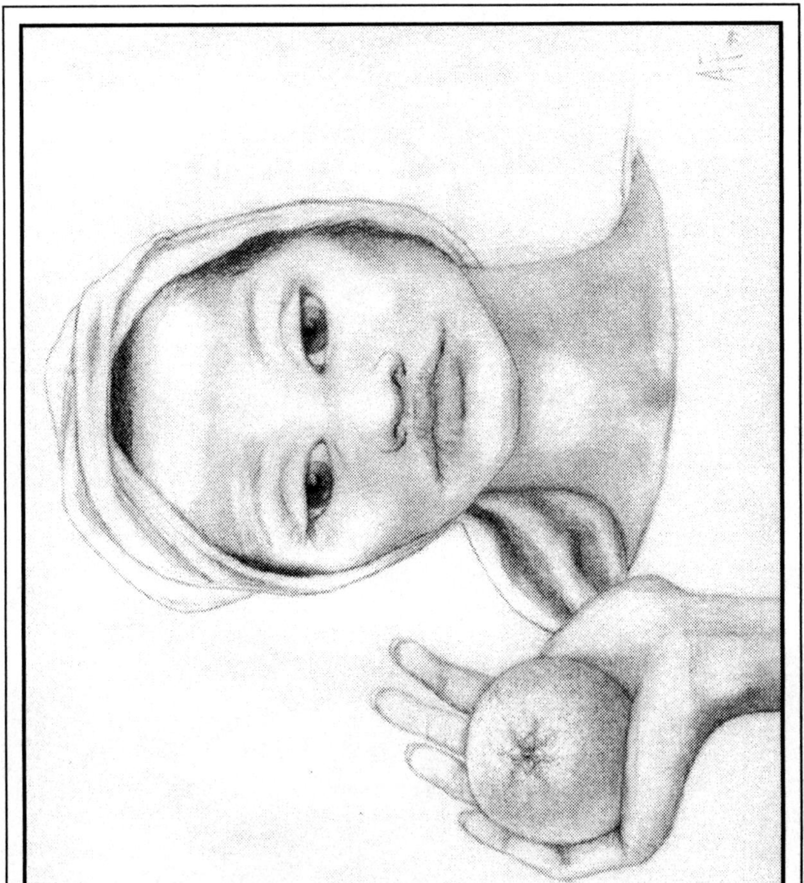

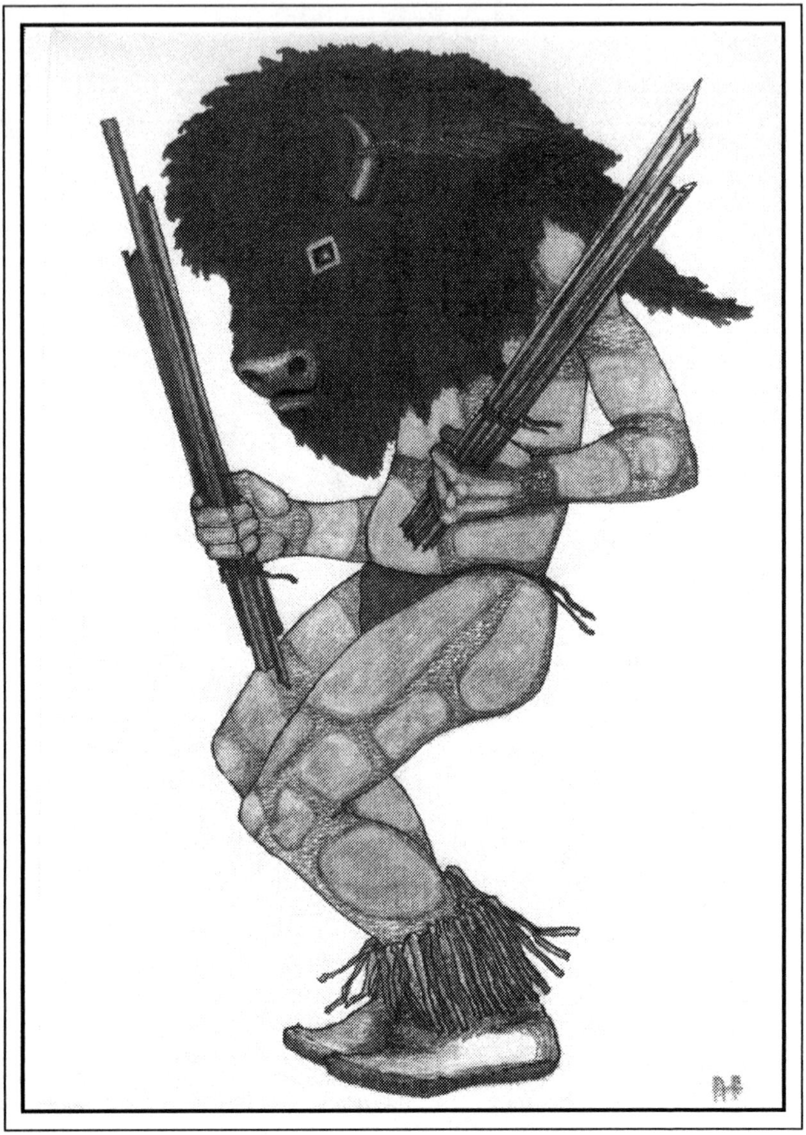

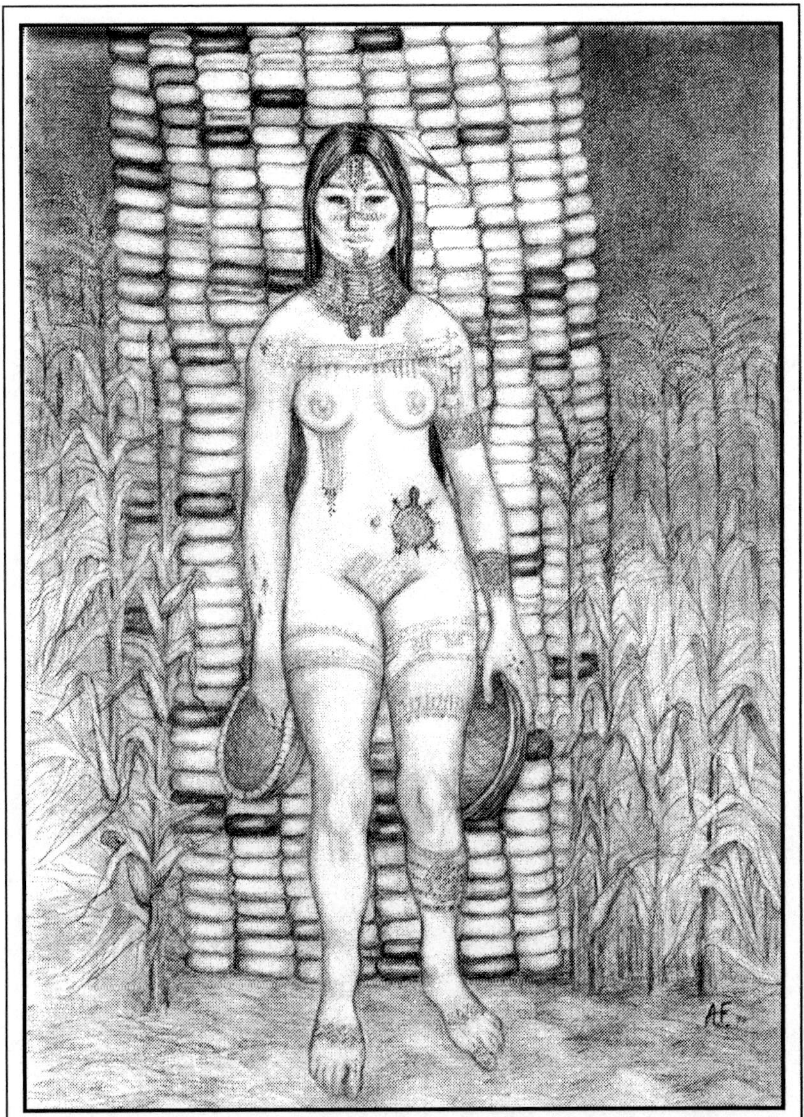
A.F.

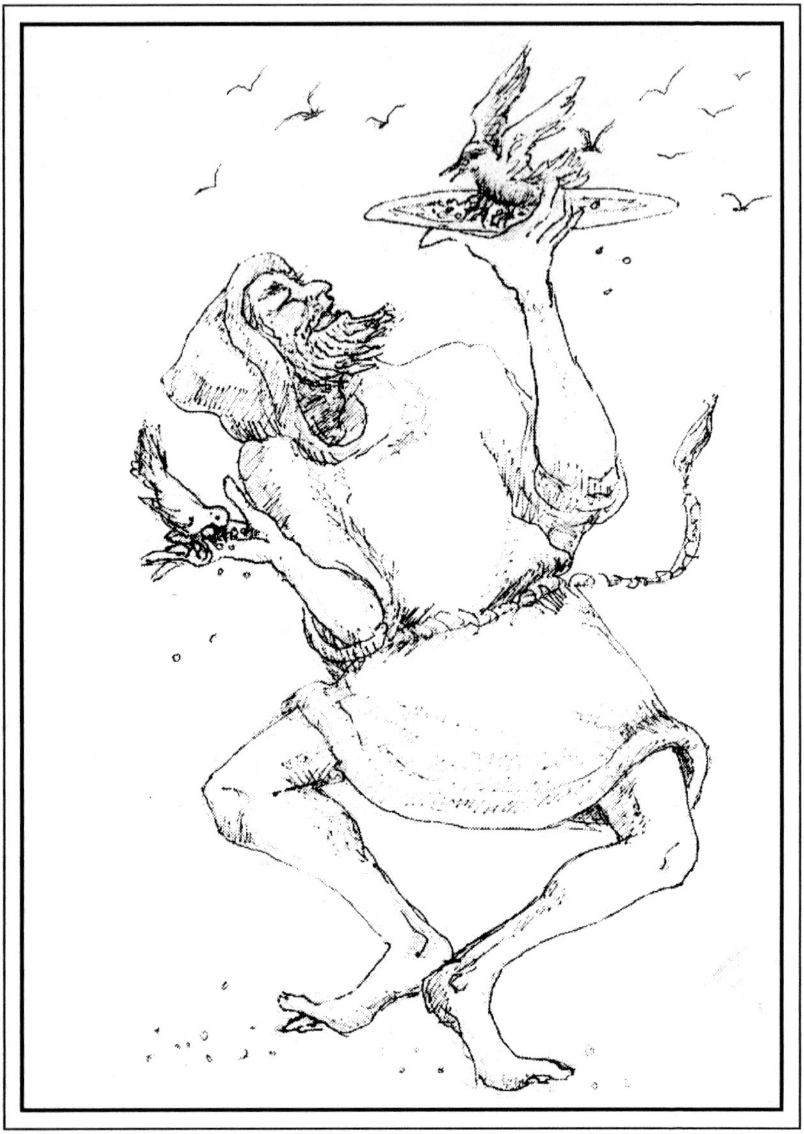

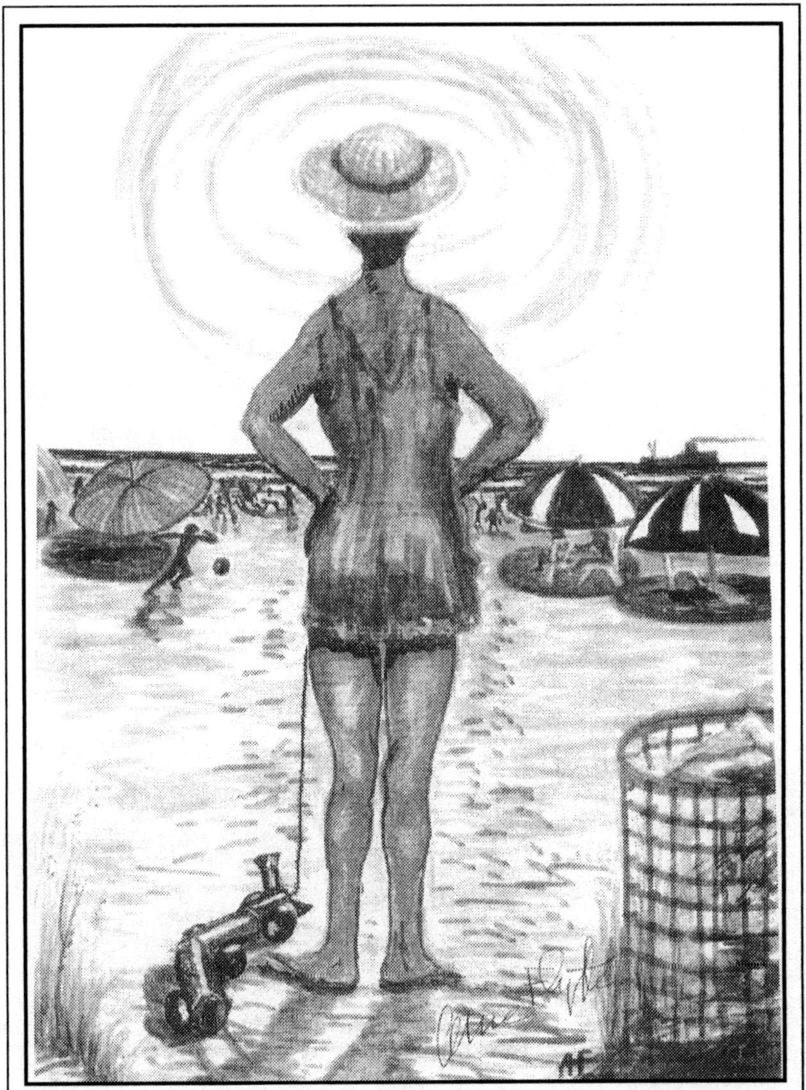

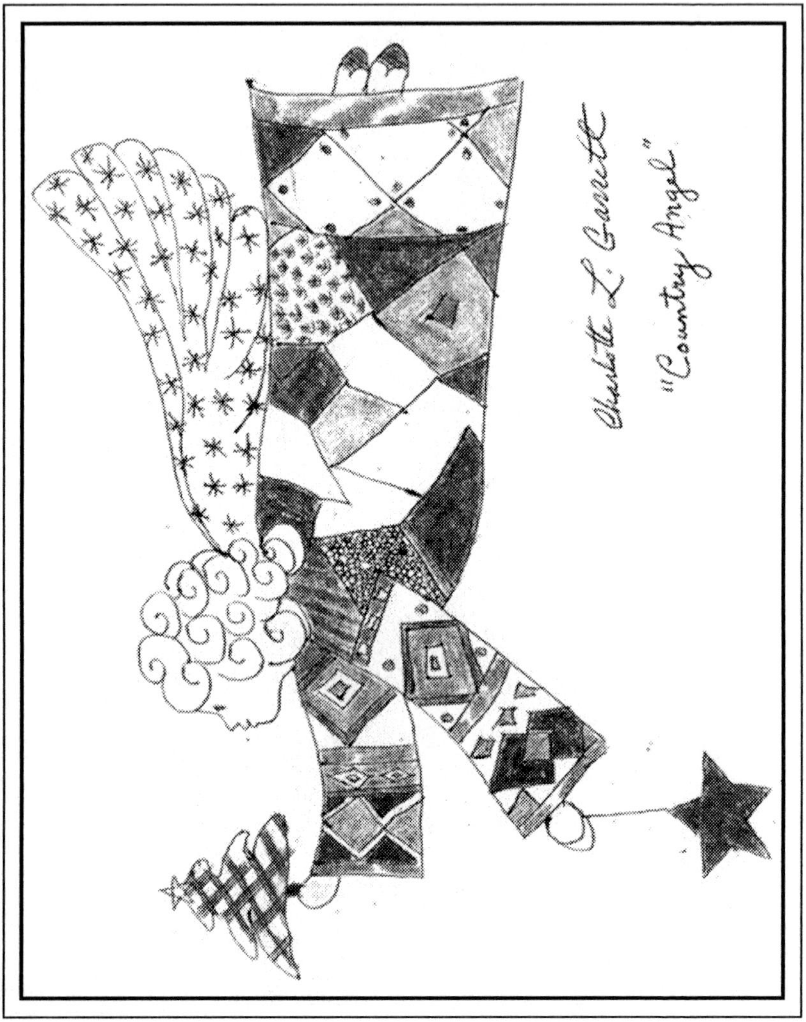
Charlotte L. Garrett
"Country Angel"

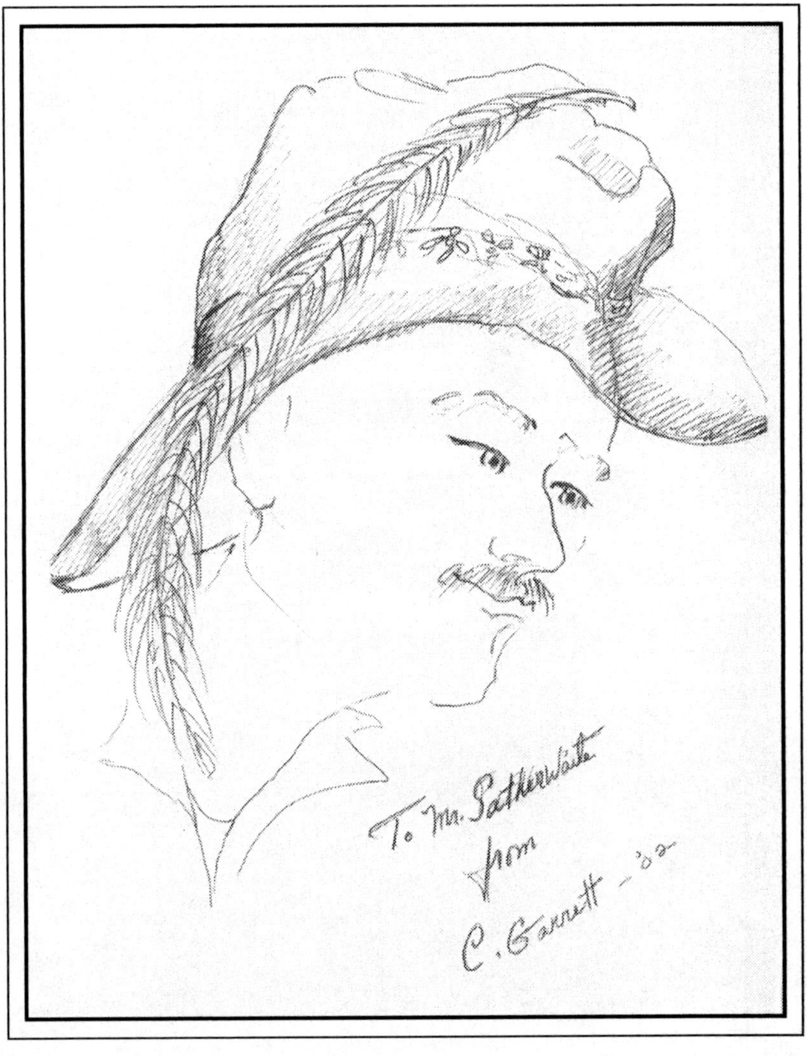
To Mr. Satterwhite
from
C. Garrett - '02

"Dear Friend, Remember..." Portrait of "Hugette Peck. 2003"

Charlotte L. Garrett

C. Garrett
'2002
Help Prevent Child Abuse –
"Cherish the Children."

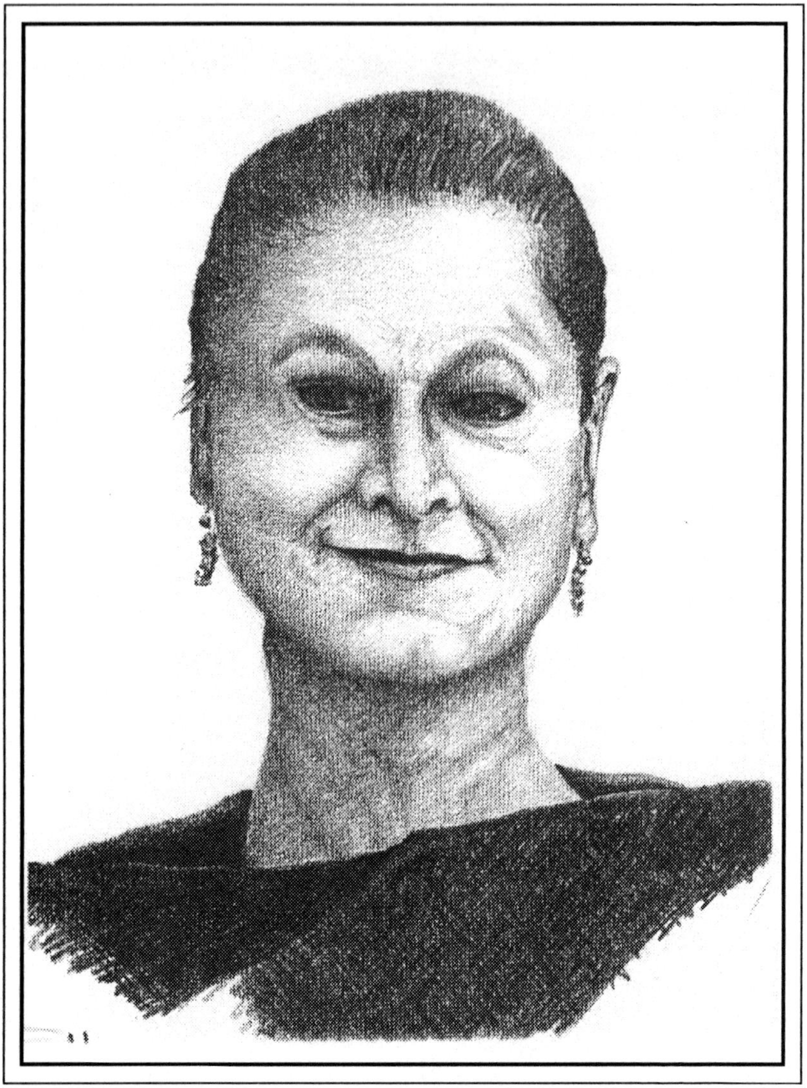

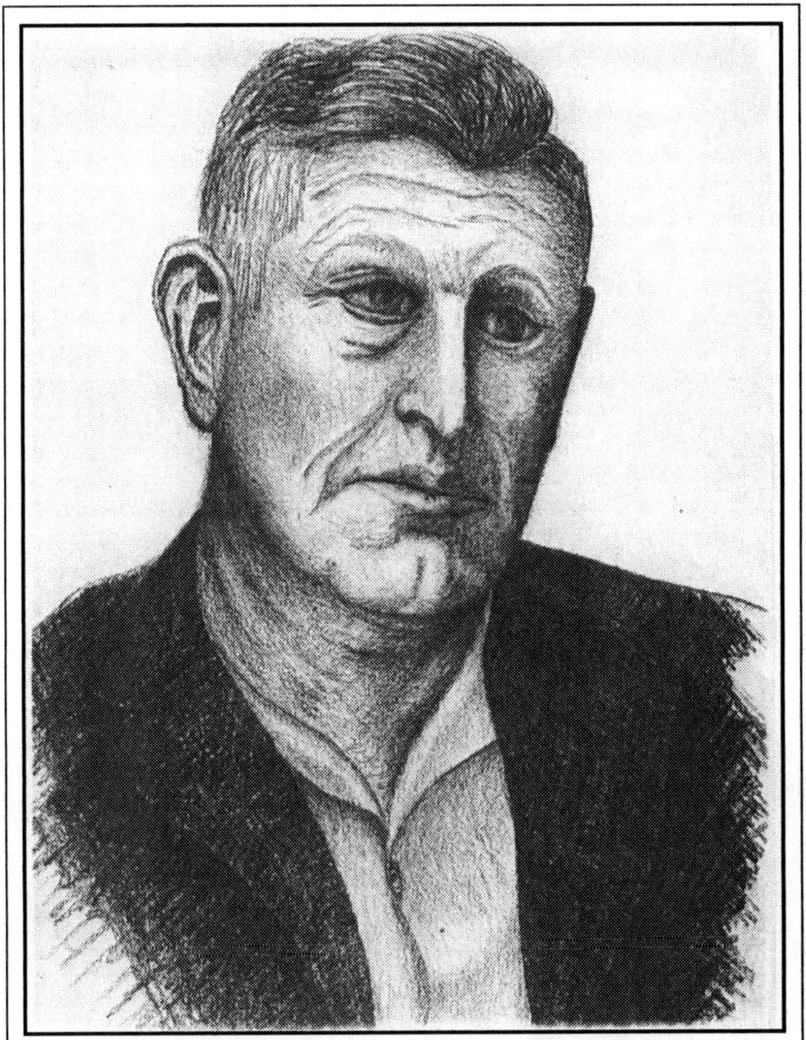

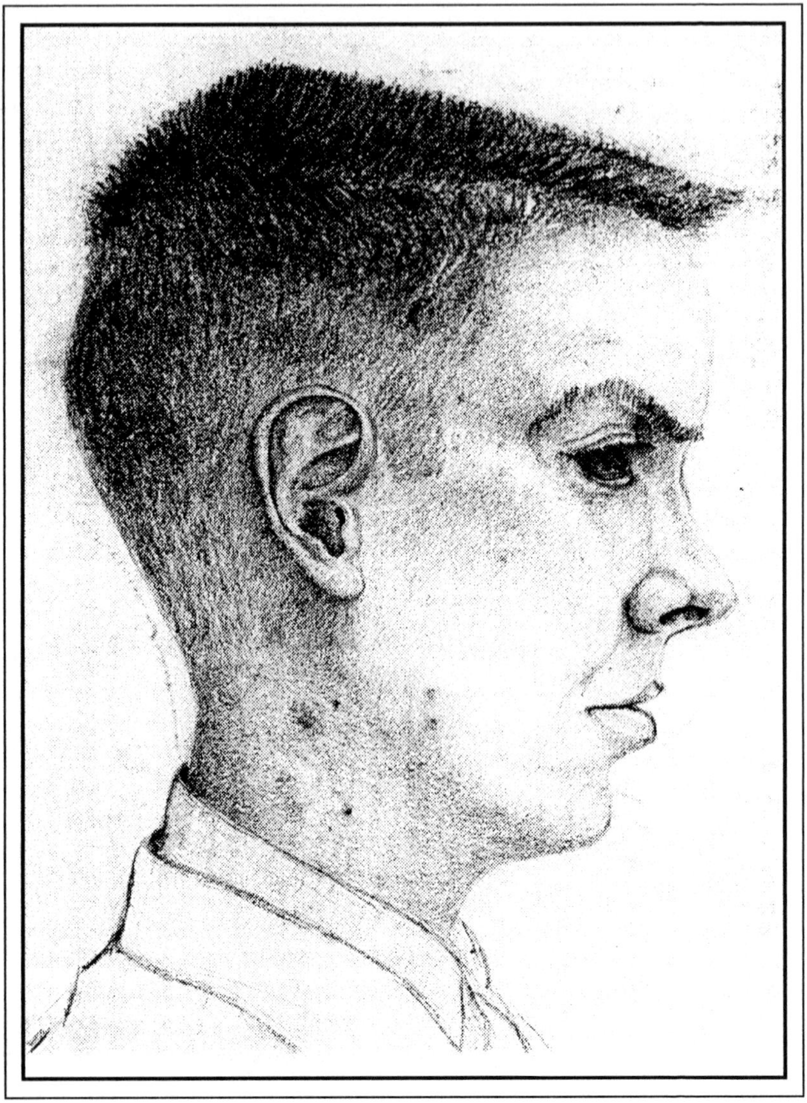

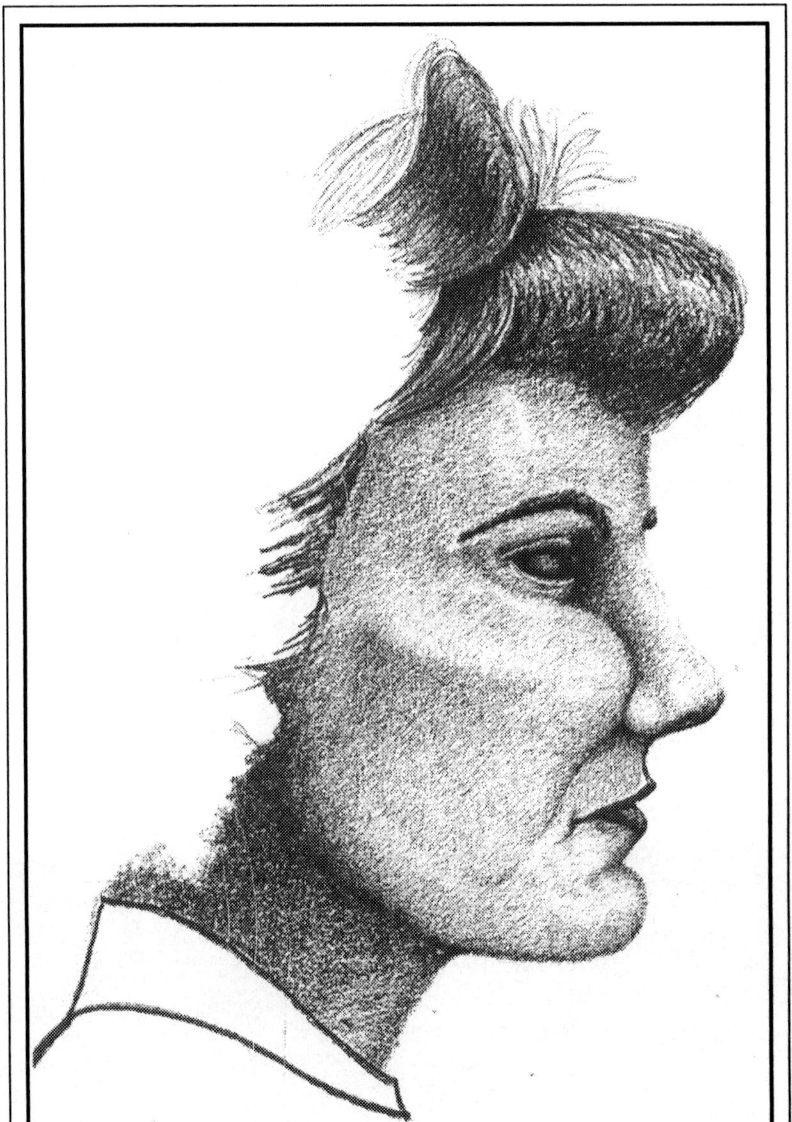

The Womb

♦

Larry Turner

It was different for us than for you.
We were adults when we were born.
Among other things, that means
we remember the womb.
Amid work, heat, cold, hunger,
pain, disease, old age, death,
we remember the womb, Eden.

It was paradise. I named the animals
and that was fun. But mostly
it was like a honeymoon that went on and on.
*That bothers you, this picture
of an intrauterine honeymoon?
I told you it was different for us.*

Like every mother since,
God grew impatient for us to emerge.
She sent the serpent among us,
who uttered three words: *There is more*,
and turned Eden from paradise to prison.

And so we left. But still,
amid work, heat, cold, hunger,
pain, disease, old age, death,
we remember the womb, Eden,
and give thanks for this world outside.

Hobson's Choice

♦

Anne Flythe

Out of a clear sky
out of smoke and fire
bodies falling like ripe fruit
past an eternity of windows.
Preternatural harvest.
Death does not usually supply
so many urgent reasons at one time
for us to welcome him
and gladly grasp his hand
as we preempt his plan.

The Other Shoe

♦

Anne Flythe

After those pyroclastic flows
rolled down the tower's shining sides
I was afraid to watch the screen,
more afraid to leave it dark.
Who knew when toy planes
might be airborne again?

Shelf Life

♦

Anne Flythe

Too high against the night
two glittering barcodes
of darks and lights
that failed to stipulate
their content or the cost
of the expiration date.

For Stuart

♦

Charlotte L. Garrett

His eyes search the middle distance
seeing a landscape vast, wide,
where time tints the canvas in shades of gold –
and only a master's brushstrokes
can transform painters' pigments
into near-breathing life and form.
Eternal waters on an imagined shore
lap sands and stones
of every beach he has walked before.
And far beyond this compelling scene,
boats and waves are gray
against cliffs reaching skyward
where mountain mists still play
about their ragged crests.
From horizon line and heavenward,
his eyes see more than mine
as we stare ahead at the same space
on our living room wall.
His vision is a landscape, vast, wide.
Mine is a portrait of his dear face
when his eyes search middle distance
for some remembered and longed-for place.
As sunlight warms my heart, paints for me
a portrait of love for my lover,
a dreamer forevermore.

Top Of The Tree

♦

Nathaniel Schellhase Hvizdos

Sordid documents reveal their dealings
Capitalizing upon ill healings
Dollars deliver us into despair
Charged regrettably here and there
With a smile it's not my fault
Payment plans that do not halt
The crucial things of law and life
Most expensive monetary strife
Working for people with cold sterile hearts
Unable to live upon love and arts
Unable to feel animalistic drive
Deep root force that say survive
Loss of ties between human and Earth
Preserved plastic frozen meals beginning at birth
They tell you its so and the TV agrees
You too can be rich if you work hard as bees
In the eve of man's forgiving
Living for money is not worth living
Lost are means of self support
Sell your labor they will purport
Lives within view amid castle walls
Feudalism brews in capitalism's halls
As hungry reach out
Non-privileged shout
Rich man abates
Militant hates
Morals collapse in the face of our nation
Fists emerge with tones of irration

With government grinding slower each day
It all returns to the matter of pay
Some will succeed and be filled with bank
Others float by depressed served and sank
And the cost of a life in the land of the free
Not much for those at the top of the tree
A lifetime for others who toil and sweat
Ending up often with regret and in debt
Angry at those who enjoy and neglect
Think of lost children with pause and reflect

Somewhere: The Evening Men
(Dedicated to all homeless people with haunted hearts)
◆

Joe Metz

On this street of faces fashioned by never-fading neon,
dimmed by marquee shade, shadows from setting towers,
lighted by pulsating stops and greens, stiff-backed street lights
waiting for time to change at dawn,
by store lights on modeled mannequins, streaming with tints
of style, by flickering lights, gasping puffs of gutter butts,
walk the evening men forward, looking back, in and out,
for Somewhere.

     "Shine on, shine on harvest moon
     up in the sky back home.
     I found a real cheap greasy spoon
     and think no more to roam."

Somewhere can be a long way,
staying bright before the tears,
having seconds on First Street,
giving age its driving time,
driving time to Hell.

Somewhere is wagging tongues,
caring lips, probing eyes,
Bible hearts, tender tones,
oven smells before dawn,
hot-water soaking showers,
crisp sheets and crazy quilts,

Saturday nights, Sunday chicken,
and the girl next door.

Somewhere is a long, lonesome
mirror of memories hoping to happen,
even for a moment more.

> "I ain't had no lovin'.
> Man, I want it all the time!
> But who's gonna give me lovin'
> for a measly, stinkin' dime?

Somewhere is the nearest alley,
down below sills rotting with plastic flowers,
down below lines of Monday's laundry,
below sounds of Saturday's sex,
below Friday's dreams of better times,
once the raise comes through.

Somewhere watches over delicatessen discards,
over piss drying on second-hand pants,
over smokes for back-alley quickies,
over fries and coke for Sunday's feast,
if the dumpsters are still serving.

Somewhere is a pathway four flights up,
around a stand of rotting stairs,
around a cold-water, dripping faucet, when the water's on,
around rusted radiators, a matted mail-order mattress
filled with dust and dreams.
Somewhere is sometimes not so far.

> "Nearer my god to thee
> than you ever were to me.
> You gave the world your only son,
> how much good you think he's done?

On this street of faces, cast down, withered up,
searching the alleys of their minds,
walk the men of evening,
wishing for dreams of someday eluding the edges of night
carved into memories chosen too quickly, too real,
blunting off the blackness of a life overcome by shadows.

In and out of spheres of time, walking on streets of hopelessness,
stumbling over curbs of hope, the men of evening watch suns dim too soon, too quietly,
walking always back in dusk, waiting for the day of light.
Somewhere a new sun rises.

> "Let us gather at a river
> made of cut-rate liquor,
> hoping with a drink or two,
> we'll get to Somewhere quicker.

(Untitled)

♦

Larry Turner

Like a quantum wave, my spirit
is not trapped within the barrier of my skin.
It tunnels out
to you
and you
and you.
Even this message
may carry it
to someone I'll never meet.

St. Brigit's Day

♦

Larry Turner

Dead tree, dead bush, field in shroud of snowy winter.
In cloudy doubt I dread to see
the worst becoming worse.
Is it my sole reward for surviving January
to be thrust into February? I
do not live by farmer's calendar,
do not watch pregnant ewes coming into milk,
do not observe days beginning to lengthen.

No, in spite of memories from past years
and prayers to you, goddess or saint,
it is an act of faith despite winter's shadow to
still believe the green of coming spring,
still celebrate tree in bud, bush in blossom,
still see myself dancing
in fields of flowers under returning sun.

Summer is Running Away

♦

Charlotte L. Garrett

Summer is running away.
We waved goodbye to her today;
she tossed her curls and laughed . . .
we heard her saying "Goodbye."
Green leaves linger with last roses, sun-hats, sandals,
bright skies, tall pines, beach grasses,
dark glasses and cool wine.
Lovers, dreamers, children, the young and old
listen to oceans, sift soft sand.
Go build all your castles
and then take her hand; love her, smile with her, sing happy
songs.
She will return again.
Summer is running away.
We waved goodbye to her today;
yet, here in my hand a seashell . . .
bewitched, I am under her spell . . .
Summer.

"In Amelia's Garden"
Charlotte L. Garrett

Promise of Spring

♦

Charlotte L. Garrett

Wake up, little garden;
send out a few flowers.
Cover bare borders and empty bowers
with something better than
brown leaves and blight.
My eyes are tired of winter white.
Where are jonquils, tulips, lilies
planted last fall?
Did chipmunks dine on them after all?
Later I can have roses to brighten my lawn
to help me greet each early dawn,
free of fungus, black spot and ants.
When will that ever be?
When Spring keeps her promise
to my little garden and me.
Waiting for the promise of Spring,
meanwhile just grow any old thing.

How And Why

♦

Nathaniel Schellhase Hvizdos

How do you save your crackhead friends
Slipping down tears
Razor's edge bends
They are taunting their death in a slow downward fall
Creeping eyes lie through friendship and all
You cannot be with them all day after day
Not knowing what promise or coercion to say
Looking away but still thinking of them
Fix yourself first
Finish coughing up phlegm
I am no good to others if I am no good to me
Must help myself unite so I will let myself be
Then in their darkness I might be a light
Give them a hand from their disastrous plight
Who needs the help
Who would give a damn
Who would smack my face for being a ham
Which one is the addict or chronic abuser
Who is erratic
A recreational user
Wanting these answers for seeking solutions
Bringing my friends into serene ablutions
Not sleeping at night and not knowing why
Thinking quite soon that you will surely die
Reading a book with a similar plot
Scatter-brained silly about that one thought
Your eye muscles sore as you settle to sleep
Distant trains roar as synaptic nodes steep

My mind has grown tired yet yearning awake
A hundred miles an hour my waking won't break
Close your eyes and unsew your lips
Unscrew the brain releasing all quips
How much farther can my mind possibly bend
I wish it would stop
I wish it would end

Melvin Beasley, Veteran

♦

Joe Metz

They never knew what I saw,
what the time was when men fought
and killed as if someone was right,
which made it just fine to fix bayonets,
lob grenades and cringe when they went off,
seeing bits and morsels of what were human
at one time but not when war is being fought.

They never knew what I knew,
that the home-town papers carried good news,
victories, boys coming home with medals,
while the trenches, jungles, tents
smelled of sweat and fear and blood,
and your buddy since basic training
zipped in a body bag waiting to be airlifted out.

They never knew what I felt
about being a soldier for three years,
about saluting the chain of command
without ever knowing whether it was
the man or his uniform with stripes and bars
that deserved our attention and right face
or just that they had survived more battles.

They never knew how I cried
when letters from home said "It's a Boy!"
but I'm on patrol sloshing through swamps
with wet boots and soggy cigarettes

wishing I could be back there right now
handing out cigars, candy, and handshakes,
laughing as my wife says, Glad you're here."

They never knew my depression
as I sat at the bar having shots with chasers,
pretending to forget that it had happened,
still hearing the shells, the sobs, the shrieks
in some small part of my memory
not numbed over by sour mash bourbon
or drowned out by a patriotic jukebox.

They never knew why I died
in an alley by a fence I'd climbed once
to get the stocking ball my cousin hit,
by a graying garage my uncle rented
by the month to park his 1943 Ford,
by the times of our lives I remembered
long before we wondered what war was.

They'll never know that I smiled
when the pain in my heart exploded.

Truncated Rainbow

♦

Larry Turner

She saw red.
Everything she wanted was tied up in red tape.
So she caught the red-eye to New York,
Determined to paint the town red.
Next day, she had not one red cent.
Worse than that, she was in the red.
It was scarcely a red-letter day for her.
So this red-blooded redneck girl
Headed for the red-light district to recoup her fortunes.
They caught her red-handed, but she declaimed,
"This is all a red herring!
I'm just a red-hot American girl having fun!"

You'll recognize her immediately as a blue-blood,
Her money all coming from blue-chip investments.
Perhaps she's even a blue-stocking, or worse
A bluenose supporter of the blue laws.
Yet once in a blue moon
On a Blue Monday when she's feeling blue,
Out of the blue
She'll show her blue-collar side,
Climb on stage, sing blues,
Maybe even pick up a banjo and play bluegrass,
Her blue-ribbon performance marking her
As a true-blue American girl having fun!

Cutting of the Grass

♦

Norma Redfern

What a wonderful day to do other things,
the sun is out, not too hot.
I lay in bed and think of all
I would rather do.
Alas, I have to cut the grass.
It grows with every drop of rain,
lush and green, trying to reach the sun,
only to be cut, then to start again.
My life revolves around the yard,
if not this week, it must be the next.
It is endless, until the Fall.
The scent of fresh-cut grass
will remain in my mind until Spring,
only to start again;
the never-ending chore of Summer:
the cutting of the grass.

Look to the New Year

♦

Norma Redfern

I don't think we treasure the time we have.
What was important about what you did last year?
As every year comes to an end, and a new one begins,
what do we have to show for what we did or did not do for others?
Time passes so quickly, and then the year has come and gone.

We grow older and what have we done?
Have we given to others as much as we have taken?
What road have we gone down only to return empty handed?
Have we taken the time to share with a loved one? Or even
thought, Do I want to be alone without someone
to share the rest of my life with?

Have we made someone in our life happy?
Or do we take others for granted,
only to walk down that road and return another year older?
Perhaps this year can be a new beginning for all of us,
reaching out, sharing with others,
making someone happy and, most of all, giving of ourselves.

Make the most of your time.
Make this a special year,
with good friends and loved ones.

Bette Davis Lies

♦

Anne Flythe

Making it this far was hard,
staying on the cusp between
old age and death may prove more difficult as
one grows reluctant to leave this scene.
Does the angle of repose apply
where the slippery slope
grows less precipitous,
where even time slows down?
Moving carefully along the ridge,
mind and eye may disagree
as to the point of no return
where down becomes inevitable.

Living with Ghosts

♦

Charlotte L. Garrett

Because they were loved
they are not gone;
memory permits them to live on,
Mother, Father, Brother, Husband,
leaving the living, their life ends.
But time and love, brief, fleeting,
hold them for awhile,
leaving me a remembered smile.
Faces and words of each one
return to catch me by surprise,
seeking my future in lifeless eyes.
I am living with ghosts,
yet I have no fear,
for they are mine,
and I hold them dear.

Happiness is not a Place

♦

Charlotte L. Garrett

Happiness is not a place,
a time, or person, not even a season.
Perhaps it is not one face,
or look, or for one special reason;
but, instead, hearts fulfilled,
content, and resting,
as do our wood-doves nesting,
calling their six-note love songs
into frozen air. No-longer-alone-doves questing,
they know Nature's secrets; no others *are* there.
Yet we search on and on
until life itself is fleeing,
then, finally, gone.

Effort

♦

Nathaniel Schellhase Hvizdos

Millions to the effort
Money
Millions to the effort
People
Millions to the effort
Weapons
Millions to the effort
Dying
Why do women cry at night
Their sons have gone off to fight
Raise another for the state
Pollute minds with nation hate
Interject for market prices
Monroe Doctrine okays vices
Guatemalan genocide
Many others Hades ride
Gun the law
No one saw
United Fruit Corporation
Sanctioned cultural mutation
Just ask Rigoberta Menchu
What does our country hide from you
Killing leaders who organize
Weekend shopping finds our prize
Bribery through legal channels
Lobbyists affecting panels
Gun the law
No one saw

Leadership
Education
Encouraging jubilation
Media nation needs a cure

Sestina for a Vagabond

♦

Joe Metz

I stalk the train yards mostly at night,
hoping there'll be open freight cars,
keeping myself in damp, dark shadows
around rusting sheds, beside the coal carriers,
listening for sounds of any footsteps
crunching along the graveled dirt.

I have memories of playing in dirt
as a kid, wishing away the night,
hoping there'd be no soft footsteps
coming to say, "Put away your cars
and trucks," taking away my carriers
of phantom freight in deepening shadows.

I live now in secret, searching for shadows,
crawling though the murk, the oily dirt,
hating these steel, stinking carriers
railing me along, day through night,
watching for the next yard, the next cars,
moving me along in my father's footsteps.

I needed his fervor, not just footsteps
stomping up our stairs in long shadows
to mend my prayers; not leaving cheap, tiny cars
with moveable parts or looking for the day's dirt
on my hands; not saying a numb, "Goodnight,"
before leaving to chase his distant carriers.

But she knew that caring, her love, were carriers
of feelings beyond motherhood; that footsteps
coming softly to bring me home before night
came shielded me from tall, lurking shadows;
that tender hands washing away the day's dirt
would join me in prayer, tuck away my cars.

I never saw him jump for handles on rolling cars,
bouncing away on a train of rattling cold carriers,
leaping desperately into the newness of distant dirt.
But fixed are my memories of her faltering footsteps,
hands grown gnarled, eyes sunken deep in shadows,
lips taut and white, praying away the night.

She died at night. I rode in her coffin-carriers,
flags on cars of anguish, wishing for her footsteps.
I ran to shadows. Steel hulks hauled my grief in their dirt.

Old Time Westerns

♦

Joe Metz

There was a time, long since past,
when with a dime you'd have a blast,
fill an afternoon with candy and fun,
watching Hopalong Cassidy tote his gun,
look at Lash LaRue cracking his whip,
or see Wild Bill Elliott aim from the hip.
It was easier then to know right from wrong:
Roy Rogers had Trigger, Gene Autry his song.
Bad guys in black hats would pillage and steal,
but got sent to Boot Hill by stony Bob Steele.
Johnny Mack Brown, with old Fuzzy Knight,
cleaned up the saloons and set sinners right,
while Tom Mix, Tim Holt, and Tex Ritter too,
rode over the screen, as heroes we knew.
When we wished for a bad guy to end up in jail,
along came the handsome and quiet Monte Hale.
Buster Crabbe (before Tarzan) rode tall in the saddle,
and much like Hoot Gibson had no time for prattle.
Now tickets are higher, our movies are stranger,
but I still like Red Ryder and adore the Lone Ranger.
You can call me old-fashioned, with memories too dim,
well face up with "The Duke" and tell that to him!

One Evening, at Least

♦

Deborah S. Snyder

in the last century was warm –
where and when
it should not have been:

in November, outside
Boston. And boys
in crew cuts and chinos, nights,

would be leaning against the lampposts
smoking, girls with them, everyone waiting
and waiting

for life to begin.
And no wind caressed them, nor
anyone else; no one felt anything, until

it rained and the treetops were speaking
of the mild breezes
in autumn.

And as I was walking even further away,
I began noticing – even at this distance
and through their picture window,

that my parents' TV was visible –
smaller, yet still
flickering, despite my anguish.

Black white gray – replaying
for hours yesterday's Dallas motorcade, replaying
in my mind my parents' shrill

silence also, as it
followed still another quarrel. Having to tiptoe,
I closed the front door,

then the storm door, believing if only
I were quiet enough, I could
undo what was done.

They had lowered
the sky, in the afternoon –
every flagpole, the color

of a tin cup. In one moment, thunder
distant – sounded like a chair
scuffing the floor, dragged by a relative

wanting to get closer to the set –
and that set my mother off. Thunder,
and this far North of

where I am living now: almost winter.
Yet, there it was again.
This time directly overhead, a floor

in heaven. Now many chairs
in a room, the world
as it was slowly streaming

out of Camelot. Yet, those times
are clear, even now: road
on a map, avoid it.

Yellow light
in the pine-paneled den; aquarium, TV,
all the picture of when

I let go of courage.
Ninth grade, and again
we had to read Frost, in the first year

Frost no longer lived. I got up –
shy, plump, clumsy; and just knowing,
everyone hates me.

So I would never speak to anyone. Nor
would I say what, or what I did not
think: *silence*

is golden. Anyway, everyone in class
was cutting up making Patti, Mary Jane,
and Geri laugh: or Howie, Ritchie,

Pete, Jimmy, and John were, at any rate.
And I wanted them to like me.
So, on a dare I started

stammering so they would laugh.
Then under my breath, as I started
back to my desk – being

sure of being
in earshot of everyone –
I whispered:

*and anyway, who
in hell cares about "The Road Not Taken,"*
or something like that. The teacher,

124

scowling, failing me would never come to
say anything to anyone: even when witnessing
me losing who I was.

Year End Prayer

♦

Larry Turner

As the year comes to an end, we thank you
for all you have done for us this year.

You have restored us to health while all over
the country our friends are suffering and dying
from diabetes and other afflictions.

With all these gifts you've given us, I hesitate to speak,
But I have some new poems that I think you'll find unique.

You have brought us here and surrounded us with beauty,
in our home, our garden, our neighborhood, our city,
and throughout our state.

I know that you're omniscient, but I'll give this little hint.
These poems that I mentioned, I would love to see in print.

You have given us a church and community
through which we may serve and be active
in doing your work.

You would not find it difficult since you made heaven and earth,
To find a publisher to print these poems of Christ's birth.

You have placed us in the midst of a loving family
who genuinely like one another.

*I know these poems may not be the kind that you'd applaud.
Of Mary and her soldier's love, a passion sent from God.*

You have provided us with this Christmas time
bringing all of this together—
the beauty, church, community, family and purposeful activity
to make a joyous season we will never forget.

*Maintaining all the Cosmos, you must have a lot to do,
So if you can't see to my poems, I guess that's okay too.*

Ribbet

♦

Anne Flythe

First, put down that wretched frog!
Do be careful when you pray or make a wish,
you may achieve your heart's desire
and live to rue the day.
All I asked for was one perfect man
to fill my heart and warm my bed.
Though I was not uncomely,
all doted on *his* handsome face,
and so it went: where I
was stumble-footed he was grace.
I never thought my imperfections
would loom a dark tsunami in contrast
to his sunlit excellence and beauty.
How gladly would I kiss my prince
to turn him frog again.
To lift the spell: a farewell salute
upon his chill brow with willing lips
that I might regain my ordinary self
and neither outshine nor be eclipsed.

Why Flora Moved To Berkeley

♦

Anne Flythe

A city girl, New Yorker born and bred,
she was disconcerted when both her urban thumbs
and all eight fingers itched with green ambition.
Until the day she dreamed a little garden
at the bottom of a sometimes sunny shaft,
almost an atrium, that lay
between two condos' barren walls.
The shallow soil, itself imported, held
one spindly golden locust tree, a hybrid
held proof against botanical disasters.
There was a shrub or two, some bulbs,
a few perennials, that's all.
Satisfied at last, she smiled;
but after nine eleven when the Towers fell,
winter came early on day nine twelve.
She woke, to find, beneath a white ash fall,
her plants well mulched with papery debris:
the remnants of efficiency refiled
among chrysanthemums and asters.
It seemed unlikely that Spring would see
her flowers bloom, thrust up through
the weight of all that's lost, especially
since the toxic smoke of hate
lingers like a killing frost.

Last Night was a Dream

♦

Charlotte L. Garrett

Last night was a dream, only a dream?
Surely it is not so,

For I heard the creaking of the swing
and I saw pale moonlight glow

on columns graceful in the light,
on pine trees stately, tall.

And I saw a young girl running
through a doorway from the hall.

Tripping lightly over the sill
she closed the screen door tight

and her summer dress, flowered, thin,
rustled her into the night.

Sweet shrub grew on the moonlit lawn,
melodies hummed through the air,

Beauty breathed in happiness
and knew that she was fair.

Her lover sat on the front porch swing;
she rushed to his side with delight,

circling white arms about his neck,
murmuring of love to the night.

How tender, warm and poignant
the kisses of the young.

It is for them, for they have love,
our sweetest songs are sung.

Bathtub Blues

♦

Nathaniel Schellhase Hvizdos

Two young brothers still bathe together
Roof and deadbolt still comes bad weather
Their water is warm but not burning hot
With cars and a frog a bathtub tot lot
Splashing and laughter
Teenager looks in
Life changes after a babysat sin
Our racing cars stop
Our eyes race in wonder
Unzipping his pants he shows us what's under
Kneeling to question
He forces a yes
Hate registration
Emotional mess
Eternal minutes and forgotten details
Re-zipping he goes left biting our nails
Tattle tale nature that very night
Mother's boyfriend's son
Strangle him
Right
He said he is sorry or so my Mom tells
Eighteen years later to console my yells
Years of forgetting slowly return
We called him our brother but now how I burn
How 'bout my brother
Godfathered his daughter
He must be deadened a sick mental slaughter
Mom still defensive

She says people change
Teenage molester societal mange
This World is too big
Her back should have turned
What good is her love when she should have spurned

Lamentations From a Fledgling Poet

♦

Joe Metz

Oh, yeah, I enjoy writing the stuff,
but what seems to me awfully tough
is finding the right word every time
to give each line a perfect rhyme.

Although it's easy with a word like "taut"
to find a rhyme with hardly a thought,
"precipice" used as an ending word,
in the poet's trade, could be quite absurd.

I use a thesaurus and a dictionary,
while telling myself, "It's not that scary!"
So a current sampling of my structured verse
shows some could be better, some might be worse.

But even sometimes, with a rhyme at hand,
I layer my stanzas with words so bland
that lovers of poets with a genius streak
must rate my English as "Extremely weak!"

But why, "A meadow resplendent housing bovines,
'Midst the verdant splendor of pastoral scenes?"
when the image I think such words should raise
is a field with some cows left out to graze.

And if "Anguish untold smites a damsel divine,"
what should I use for the very next line:
"Soon she shall hearken to a call from the brink?"
or, "She'd soon better see a reputable shrink?"

Now the lines, "His descent into Lucifer's realm,
O'er the river Styx with Death at the helm,"
might lead on to a story with a moral to tell,
or, "Some guy just died and went straight down to Hell."

Well, that's my dilemma as a poet-in-training:
to say it right out or sound like I'm straining?
To be cleverly turgid like masters of verse,
or churn out my lines all tepid and terse?

So surely you see I feel poetry's charm
and sense how I versify in a state of alarm.
I guess my career is balanced on a precipice,
and only time will tell if I've made a real mess of it.

The Man Next Door

♦

Larry Turner

*According to this newspaper
the man next door just bit the dust.
Throw out his trash. Open the window.
Let in the air and light of day.
Tear out that moldy linoleum.
How long he's been here I forget.*

How long I've been here I forget.
I'll find the date from newspapers
stacked there on the linoleum,
but not now. It might start the dust
motes dancing in the light of day
that struggles through the dingy window.

I mostly avoid the window.
It's summer? Winter? I forget.
The all too brilliant light of day
annoys my eyes. My newspapers
show me the world. I'll mop the dust—
tomorrow—from the linoleum.

A rat crosses the linoleum.
Drafts rattle the window,
chill the room, disturb the dust.
Friends and family all forget
I'm here. I shiver under newspapers.
Will I see tomorrow's light of day?

My eyes are stabbed by light of day
reflecting off linoleum.
I'll paste old newspapers
over the front and back windows.
And something else that I forget—
Oh, yes, tomorrow I must dust.

Oh, yes, tomorrow I shall dust,
wash windows, see the light of day.
I'll buy new clothes. I won't forget.
I'm tired of this linoleum.
Why is there paper on the windows?
I'll cart away these newspapers.

Dust lies thick on linoleum.
Light of day at opaque windows
forgets this body amid newspapers.

Convoys, 1942

♦

Charlotte L. Garrett

It became an odd game:
watching the trucks roll by
carrying the soldiers away, away –
to the war, to violence, pain
endurance, the physical witnessing of death, to places
beyond the real, the known,
comfort, the beautiful, too far.
Some will not return;
and not even one will ever be the same.
Two little girls on the side of the road
waving to soldiers, smiling, waving to boys
not much older than themselves,
giggling if a few wave, whistle.
Among all those soldiers
will any remember
two little girls on the side of the road?

Ink and Paper

♦

Charlotte L. Garrett

Smooth, white paper, with lines luring my pen,
daring me to put down words, to draw pictures,
to express myself.
What fun it should be.
Why then do I hesitate?
It is the old, ever vigilant inner-censor telling me to wait,
not to reveal my thoughts;
they sometimes come back unwanted when re-read,
after the passage of time.
But this tempting blankness overcomes my hesitation.
Just as I would enjoy putting footsteps
on an empty stretch of beach,
so I write.

Good People Everywhere

♦

Nathaniel Schellhase Hvizdos

Waterlogged a sluggish state
Money bogged with public late
Build brand new schools for suburb fools
Cramped city kids must stretch their lids
Tainted people at all levels just how the pumpkin's carved
Clean it up remove all devils
Our sights are slowly starved
A little mess we'll clean it up
Population distance
Fifteen percent back to your cup just a copulation instance
From eminent decay paint falling everyday
Slat drapes are always drawn fluorescent dying lawn
Number one the light
Treat the children right
Number one the light
Treat the children right
Medicinal bong hits before breakfast
Bullets before noon
Close the door is now the swoon
See the cops and bullet holes
An uzi on the phone she knows
Glass dick condos through cut chain link
Vans of sorrow wearily stink
Alley treasures piled galore
Turn the corner slinks a whore
Up the street tall dude talkers
Jazz old area turned to stalkers
Glare and blur but watch behind

Look in cracks to catch a find
Mental candy
Good oppression
Go to church and learn a lesson

Stone

♦

Nathaniel Schellhase Hvizdos

The rough rock lay limp
Lifeless on the ocean floor
Turning white with age

The Second Coming: A Second Opinion

♦

Joe Metz

O.K., look. Why even bother?
I mean, it's all right there in plain sight.
If even the fallen sparrow
hardly gets no more than a quick glance,
why come back for a second go at it?
Let's be honest here!
How can it not be obvious,
you know, to a man like yourself,
that atoning for our sins,
trying to be the real good savior,
hasn't slowed us down a whole lot.

Go ahead, man. Pick any commandment.
Any one you like. And you know what?
I bet you as we speak, like right now,
somebody, hell, lots of people all over
are breaking it all to pieces!

Now pick yourself some cause.
Something like you in that temple.
You like to bet again that, you know,
some moneychanger still gets it off with
"I win! You lose! Tough shit!"

You're saying what?
The cross was a heavy-duty act?
They didn't understand. Right?

Not much compassion. Right?
Lots of fantasy faith. Right?

Hey, count on a lot more this time.
It's like, if you hear what I'm saying,
we got a real mean multitude out there.

Now, it'd be great having you back.
With your bag of miracles and quick fixes,
well, Jesus man, we'd make a fortune!
You know, coming out with T-shirts,
posters, TV clips, autographed blessings.
And, imagine this now. 'Apostle Amulets,' with healing
power for a full twelve months.
What? Well, yeah. How about a month for free and we'd
take out the 'Judas' one?

O.K., let's just skip all the business stuff.
It can come later. I mean, only if you do.
Now, like I've been asking all along,
why do this return trip thing anyhow?
You got the kingdom. Right?
You got the power. Right?
You got the glory. Right?
Well, maybe that's as good as it'll ever get.

But, hey, I'm trying to be honest here.
You need to come back? Then do it man!
But, for Christ's sake, you know, your sake,
don't get careless again. Keep it cool.
Like under control. You know what I mean?
This time there'll be a lot more of us here banking on you.

Ground Zero

♦

Larry Turner

This dome topping some
regional trade center became the
symbol of the twentieth century only
because it was so well constructed it
remained standing while all else
on surrounding acres was swept away
that morning the first atomic bomb
to fall from the sky
exploded above it.

The terms Paleozoic, Mesozoic, Neozoic
were judged too advanced for fifth-graders,
so the textbook called them
The Era of Ancient Life,
The Era of Middle Life,
The Era of Modern Life.
To these, our teacher Mrs. Keck told us,
we must now add The Atomic Age.
How could she be so far-seeing?

The blast tearing a hole in the very air of Hiroshima
ripped history in two more than anything
since the BC/AD divide.
Compared with this:
The killings of Hitler, Stalin, Mao?
Just more of the same.
Pearl Harbor?
Just another battle.

Nine/Eleven?
Just another murder.

Along with buildings and persons below,
the blast obliterated any
rationale for war as instrument
of national policy, any credibility for
claims of national sovereignty.
What Mrs. Keck grasped so quickly,
so many leaders still haven't learned.

They Called Him Crowbar

♦

Nathaniel Schellhase Hvizdos

My Grandpa's name is Walter Schrass
He likes to drink and not grab ass
A great card player who could shake a leg
Dancing on the table while we tap the keg
He took us to the park where they had dolphins and seals
Ask all the ladies he's got sex appeal
But never did he cheat 'cause he's a pious man
Could drink ten beers before he hit the can
Was in the Army during World War Two
Then to the Post Office to help me and you
Walter Joseph Schrass the First
He had four kids and one is my Mom
Maybe that's why he's got the cool calm
He built his own tiered garden
That was what he grew his flowers in
He cuts the grass yeah mows the lawn
Then drinks a Manhattan to get it on
Smoked cigarettes but quit one day
Before each meal he likes to pray
He likes to wear hats and get real crazy
He had two sisters Louella and Mazie
With a brother named Jim who I never met
He'd tie you up in the basement if you got him upset
Walter Joseph Schrass the First
Now his three sons are Walter Jack and Jay
Well Walter Jack and Jay moved away
Yeah moved away but then Jack came back
He doesn't live far from our dear Pap Pap

Pap Pap's what we call our grandpa
He could sew a quilt like you never saw
He also made Christmas ornaments
His life is like a tournament
Trying to be better with every clock tick
Now he's in the hospital really really sick
We all come to visit and hold his hand
This seems to be his final stand
Walter Joseph Schrass the First
Now he's gone and it makes me think
Are we not all on the brink
I went and paid my last respects
I looked around and I was vexed
Children played while people cried
On One Eighteen our Pap Pap died
We all laughed with talk of French Crick
And fireplace memories he built out of brick
Cousins siblings parents and friends
I swear right now to make amends
We'll miss you a lot and never forget
Ante up
Place your bet
Walter Joseph Schrass the First

Judas

♦

Joe Metz

I don't understand why I'm tagged as a recreant.
Just tell me now, what's so new about betrayal?
I fingered a person who dallied with Roman law,
wreaked havoc at the Temple, promoted God
as the only salvation for a world of sinners,
then sat down for a dinner of bread and wine.

Yes, of course I had a glass or two of his wine.
Yes, I heard him accuse one of us as a recreant
apostle. But think about it. With so many sinners,
it seems unfair to dote on my simple betrayal.
If somebody told you he was the Son of God,
wouldn't you consider turning him in to the law?

Should I feel I broke some divinely-given law
because I couldn't taste his blood in my wine,
feel his pain in my bread? I mean, by God,
I did hang around for a final, some say "recreant,"
kiss. As for the silver pieces causing the betrayal,
I'd guess people have taken less to become sinners.

Listen, you think I'm a sinner among sinners,
a Judas who ran to the priests and the law.
But let me tell you something about a betrayal
which had nothing to do with Eucharist wine
or an easy guess about "Who's the recreant?"
Let me tell you about a guileful Son of God.

Now please remember I was a man of God.
I was chosen to heal, to walk among sinners,
to bring peace, love, understanding to recreant
believers who had little grasp of God's law.
He sent me, Jesus knows, to share food and wine
with peasants, to preach love in times of betrayal.

Jesus knew he'd pick me out for this betrayal.
Don't you remember his communion with God?
Why wait till the last minute, over bread and wine,
to divine salvation's lure and the devil in sinners?
He knew all along about my scrapes with the law.
He knew, for his glory, I was his chosen recreant.

History damned my betrayal, casting me as a recreant
who sold the Son of God. But think of clerical law - -
sharing bread and wine, blessing the hearts of sinners.

My First Sonnets

♦

Joe Metz

My early sonnets fell short of fine art;
they lacked some iambic pentameters.
But now with resolve for doing my part,
I'm learning the rhyming parameters.
I know that the "a's", are followed with "b's",
all for achieving a good formal style;
but now is it "b", or start with the "c's"?
Getting this rhyme scheme will take me a while!
I sit and think, in my consternation,
if bards well-known , like Shakespeare and Spenser,
penned sonnets with ease, filled with elation,
or got, sometimes, real bitchy and tenser?
   If too many critics hold back their nods,
   To hell with these sonnets! I'll write ballades.

A Day Without You

♦

Norma Redfern

The small things, the things we take for granted,
time spent, a touch of the hand, a smile.
I miss so many things when you aren't here.
The scent of your skin after you shave in the morning,
sitting at the table sipping coffee,
as you tell me your plans for the day.

Garden For My Friend

♦

Norma Redfern

A gift of love from soil and seeds
to feed the needs of thee.
With love we till the soil we seed,
with rain and sun that fills a need.
Tiny sprouts, in shades of green,
each day how things will change.
Loving hands to work the soil,
what pleasure in the growing from a seed.
To fill my heart with love for thee.

Valentine

♦

Norma Redfern

Virtue is what I seek,
A love stronger than life itself.
Loving you with all my soul,
Even when you break my heart,
Now we are committed to each other,
To a lifetime of love and trust,
Insight to guide us both
Now and forever more,
Everlasting in our love for each other.

Talking Head Job

♦

Anne Flythe

Making love to the microphone,
her lower lip, a ripe red
strawberry, invites a taste.
Eyes, empty as a taxidermist's glass,
set in a mobile face
whose contradictions
are inherent.
Warmth and promise
in her practiced voice;
like any other whore
her mouth's for sale.
The media pimps will take their cut
until she grows too stale
to seduce us anymore.

Bitter Half

♦

Anne Flythe

In the early years
you never felt you lived alone.
When did it start?
With the brittling of your bones,
the hollowing of your heart,
the feeling that you loved alone?
Or was it in the moment that,
despite the ritual wishes spoken,
when a bone was broken
between the two of you,
left in your hand was only half the bone,
the smaller half, always
the wrong half.
Then you must have known
you had in fact
only half a life to call your own.

Excerpt From a Pillow Book

◆

Anne Flythe

When you left
There was no need
To step upon the singing board,
Broken moonlight
Bright shards of love
Ringing in our empty chamber
Informed my heart.

Twenty Nine Drops Of Oil In The Soup

♦

Nathaniel Schellhase Hvizdos

I've got this idea
It is not a happy thing
Not a sad thing
It is an impartial idea
Heat outside
Cold inside
Somewhere in the middle is ancient cave life
In those days life was different
Stone tools
Mud or grass huts
And then metal
Now computers
All this history
Some written
Some anthropological discovery
Cloning now
When do we draw the line before we no longer can
This line
Live simpler lives
Retreat from technology
Those of us who are troubled get hospitalized
Put on medication
Said to be dangerous
Mentally ill
Handcuffed
Sure the pills help
But why aren't we medicating the military

Trained to kill
Politically correct
Hmmm
To defend
Liberty
Justice
Freedom
The yawning cat
Lost in boredom
And fish
They never sleep
Can you imagine
A flash in the pan
Another picture in the can
Dig it
Dude
Man
Woman
Will not stop
Where is my there
Who is my us
Cut my hair
Tattoo my back
Roll a cigarette onto an escalator
Escalate
Aaah
Another gun
Another bullet
Blood spilled
Go
Join the great abliss
Yeah the great abyss of bliss
Can barely relate
Living on machines
Record your life
Real life dreams
Life without strife
I have aspirations

Don't just want to be rich
though it would be great
Positive Irie
Just working out how to be me
Flowing into tranquility
This overcomes
Nature enjoyable
Justice a court
Games are played on courts
Dear Sir
Dear Madame
I have something to tell you
Days ago your spouse died
I am so sorry
Here
Now
Pain screams out
They embrace
Bugs fly
I cry
Another sheep freezes from being sheered
Exposed it cries
It dies
Dog food
Pig bacon
Calf veal
Egg caviar
Cow ribs
I got dibs
Pass another apple
Another cold stew
A chicken for a friend
He will not tell I defend
We live with faults
Eventually we expose ourselves
Blossom and shrivel or be a new season
A seed
A tree from a seed

Our Earth cilia
Increasing surface area
This whole project
I have stopped the tape
Played the record
And spun the compact disc
My friends have a new baby
We don't see each other enough
Post your notice
Two weeks
Thirty days
And you are out
I am on an elevator
Elevate
Climb a mountain
Swim the sea
Get down
Sit
Ponder
Listen to the echo yonder
Feel your mind
But please
Help us from destroying us
Us you ask
Everything

Symbionts

♦

Anne Flythe

I tasted the pulses in
the hollows of your neck.
Your throat and lips were
cool and salty,
your mouth and tongue hot,
fresh water sweet. Your
warm hands splayed and strong
about my waist held us
weightless as astronauts
floating in midspace,
clinging wordless.
If life did start
in some shallow tidal pool,
as nameless organisms touched
and clung in fluid union
choosing to be one,
foregoing mutual destruction.
As with us, the cost
a certain surrendering of self.
We are not so different,
have discovered nothing new,
except a need to call such fusion love.

Cats

♦

Joe Metz

Cats:
demure,
secretive,
enigmatic,
lackadaisical,
snooping with silent feet,
heaving hairballs on prized rugs,
tattering curtains just for sport,
sleeping on the Chippendale table,
purring gently after a hard day's work.

Estate of Mind

♦

Anne Flythe

Muddy grassless ruts, car traveled since the last snowfall,
wind past the small abandoned house, its old tin roof
red as Georgia clay.
Pairs of windows - - wide open eyes
wooden brows lifted in surprise
to be reclaimed by city folk.
Inside, one transparent snake skin
artfully snagged and shed among the splintery debris,
a phoebe's nest built into the folds of faded cloth
peg hung on a wall.
Swirling within the shafts of sunlight,
glittering dust motes create a snow globe of
the empty room.
No one home to warn the flatlanders of the cost in lonely
living in the crow haunted landscape;
clever dark predators who speak harshly and often
breaking winter silence with purely local news.
Low blue mountains shoulder up out of the valley floor.
There must be a strong and constant run
between this home place and those wooded hills.
Splashes of snow like bird lime
linger in the rough brown yard.
If there are flowers, bulbs, in the frozen ground
only the old ones know, they who left defeated
by a future they could no longer see or comprehend.
They would have warned of hateful winds breathing failure
through the cracks and down the chimney's long cold throat.

She could have named for them the lilacs from Aunt Verna's place
and the old daffodils, scrambled eggs she called them,
dependable Spring gold from Gramma's yard.
He, gently rubbing big knuckled hands together, would have bragged as
how they had them some of the finest water hereabouts.
If the water veins still flow in the stonewalled darkness of the well,
there's cold sweet crystal on a hot day.
No one is left to tell the strangers where to look
for the Damsons and the Seckel pear.
The peach trees are long gone of course;
oaks and apple trees are planted for
grandchildren, a peach tree is planted for one's self.
No one to tell them to listen in the dusty rooms
for echoes of the lives that flourished
for awhile, like the garden - - pole beans, English peas, and squash,
the small cucumbers for pickling,
given over now to burdock and bindweed.
Both could have named the year, the month, the day
their restless young migrated with the geese
and after, pretty much stayed away;
although the geese return each spring, but not to stay.
These foreigners can create worlds,
fill them with memories and prophecies,
with people, both real and conjured up.
All in all it is a good site still, a place to come to more real and nourishing
than where they were.
Their agent, a local boy, early on had fled to town to escape hardscrabble
living; he later told his wife the buyers didn't have good sense.
Repeating like a record that needs nudging –
"just needs a little fixing up and you

got you a real cozy place with all the peace and quiet anyone
could ask for.
Am I right? or what? A real bargain,"
as though The Donald would want to add it
to his empire.
Privately he shuddered at the memory of glacial winds and
aching hands,
of Saharan summers, of dust and biting flies.
In his business he'd told his share of lies
and thought he'd seldom told a bigger one.
He worried that they'd change their minds;
his smiles grew so insincere as to be insulting,
his style pure snake oil.
He didn't know that poets could hang a sun to warm an icy
azure sky,
could raise against the dark a white and radiant moon
bright enough to read by.
Poets may weary of a place, but they move on only if they
run out of
words or worlds.

Moraine

♦

Anne Flythe

Incursive seas move inland
year by year;
somewhere along the coast
a road is lost;
the salted soil will
change allegiance to
sea wrack and tide,
forget the dreaming
greens without regret.

Wind enough, and rain,
will dull the cutting edge
of Everest;
grain by grain,
it will subside
beneath the insistent air
to rounded impotence.

I bear the glacial
weight of you;
when you prevail,
grind me to a different
and unwelcome shape,
I am the road lost,
the mountain leveled,
the self failed.

Running Away

♦

Charlotte L. Garrett

Running away, uphill, down,
running, fleeing, around, around –
panting, laughing, breathing stops.
Gasp again, my heart it hops
in half-happy beats of racing time
in rhythm with a pulsing rhyme
that speaks to me of faithfulness;
it stops.
Speak again, remind me truly,
never leave me so unruly
that I'm blind to Truth's sweet reason,
empty, lonely, longing vaguely
to betray all past endeavor,
with my better self to sever
all memory of a calmer season.
Bitter drink of realism, let me see instead
a prism,
beautiful, sparkling, beyond compare –
let it show the sun, the air.
Let my thirst at last find rest
with the better and the best.
Let my lips seek the vine,
find the cooling green grape wine,
then the kiss that follows dust,
rain in my face, wash away lust.
Look again, little coquette,
learn to walk without regret
among these hills that shelter you
from yourself, your much ado.

See the present silly pace,
running, rushing, but what's the race?
Against the clock inside or out?
Why the worry, why the pout?
Youth is young and laughing still,
you must walk now up that hill,
not hand in hand in breathless glee
but slowly, smiling, so they see
not how foolish but how wise
is the heart that speaks through eyes
tearing sometimes, laughing still,
loving every step uphill.
But touch me once again and I
surely need not walk but fly –
cannot rest, cannot be
any but a running me.

As

♦

Nathaniel Schellhase Hvizdos

As a child I never found focus
All their teachings hocus pocus
I laughed
I cried
Why was I being denied
Now an adult fulfillment I seek
Always around the bend just a peek
Not belonging
No Dad I had
Masking feelings
Marbled mad
Someday soon the rising sun
It will be mine
Magnetic time
What do you know
What do you care
Did you know I used to have hair
What do you know
What do you care
If you did then you'd be there
Tossing and turning
Nervousness burning
Needing to touch
Is that too much
Moving along
Moving along

Endlessly what is wrong
My path it keeps dividing
Left alone
Always hiding

Alive?

♦

Nathaniel Schellhase Hvizdos

Dead dead dead
I think I am dead
But my heart is still beating
And I have thoughts in my head

Holy Mother

♦

Charlotte L. Garrett

Holy Mother, hear my song.
I've been lost, I've been wrong.
Far I've wandered, far from Thee,
'cross many lands, across the sea.
Won't you let me lay my head
against your loving heart
where I may rest until you've said
we nevermore will part?
Life is brief, and Time is long –
Holy Mother, hear my song.
Mother, I have done my best;
kiss me now and let me rest.
When at last I find my home,
tell me then no more to roam,
for I am longing now to be
with my Father and with Thee.
Holy Mother, hear my song.
I've been lost, I've been wrong.
Far I've wandered, far from Thee,
'cross many lands, across the sea.

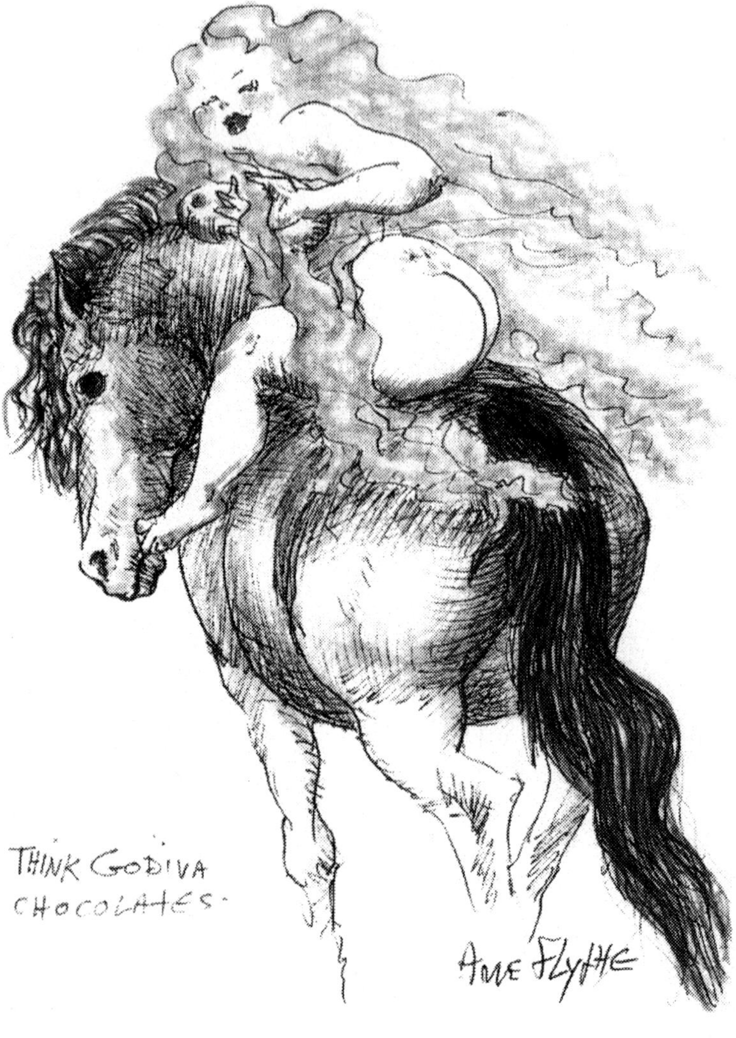
THINK GODIVA
CHOCOLATES.

About the Contributors:

Anne Heard Flythe comes from a Navy family, attending many schools yet managing to win both the senior art and poetry prizes. Since then, writing has been a lifelong pleasure, while the background in the creative arts may account for her tendency to "paint" her poems. She and her late husband, a newspaperman, lived in Washington DC for many years; they had a long good marriage and two great sons. Around 1980 they moved to "Rebel Yell," their tree farm in Spotsylvania, where Anne still lives with an Airedale named Maggie Thatcher, two volunteer cats and several guns. "I have both a permit and an attitude." Being asked to contribute to both the Riverside Writers anthology and that of the FCCA is very special to her; both groups have been excellent teachers with support and critiques.

Peter Frederick has devoted almost twenty years to his passion for photography. He took formal course work at Mary Washington College and at NOVA in Woodbridge and has been experimenting with new techniques in fine arts photography ever since. He specializes in black and white, doing his own developing and printing along with matting and framing. A frequent exhibitor at the FCCA, he has also entered works in other venues around Virginia. Peter is currently serving as curator of juried shows at the FCCA, promoting art center exhibits and greater participations in the events sponsored by FCCA.

Charlotte L. Garrett writes, "My love of painting, music and literature goes back to my school years in South Carolina when teachers and family gave support to those interests. As a young adult in New York City, I studied with professional artists who encouraged me to continue my studies. Through the years I have continued to paint—mostly portraits, figure drawings and still-life—and to write poetry and prose. Seeing an important link among poets, painters, sculptors, photographers, musicians, actors and dancers who inspire and are inspired by the works of each other, I continue to write, draw, paint and encourage others to participate in the exciting and rewarding world of art."

Nathaniel Schellhase Hvizdos writes, "I began writing poetry in my early school years, but truly began in the fall of 1993. Since then I have written thousands of poems. In 1997, during a time of crisis in my life, I lost all of my poetry composed up to then. With a name that means Gift of God Schoolhouse Star and the memory of a third-grade poem locked in my head, I began writing again and have not stopped since. My poems are reflections of everyday life and my inner relationship with God. These selections are dedicated to my grandfather, Walter Joseph Schrass the First, who once told me: Never grow old."

Joe Metz wrote his first poem when he was thirteen. Lamenting someone's "scarlet, bulbous nose," it got lost in a housecleaning binge before his fourteenth birthday. Nevertheless his fascination with writing, with intertwining fact, fiction, and feelings has never been lost.

Spending most of his professional career in various college or university settings, Joe had ample opportunities for putting words to paper. Unfortunately, this was seldom done in the name of literary creativity. Since his retirement, he has found the time he needed, the inspiration he wanted, to generate a collection of short stories, poetry by the reams, and a commitment to enhancing his creative talents. He is also committed to becoming a Master Gardener.

Joe is a member of various writing and critique groups. He lives in Spotsylvania, Virginia, with his wife, Susan. They share the rural atmosphere there with a dog, a cat, and enough growing plants to open their own nursery.

Norma Redfern is proprietor of Redfern and Sons on Caroline Street in Fredericksburg. A member of Riverside Writers, she writes poems and children's stories. She says of her creative efforts, "I write to express what others would not hear; thoughts and feeling that go unspoken. Passion, love, hope, and joy to all who read my words."

Deborah S. Snyder, MFA (Creative Writing) currently spends most of her time with her family. She has taken time off from community college teaching, just to be with them. She is now independently poor, as she was earlier in this millennium as an adjunct faculty member. To be useful these days, she sorts socks, plans meals, drives her teenaged daughter to soccer and elsewhere, walks the dog, feeds the dog, grooms the dog, paints furniture, stains cabinets, hangs pictures, swims, exercises, reads, and on good days maxes out the credit cards—she never was good at multi-tasking. She writes a monthly column for the Stafford Sun on county issues, events and people. Beginning in August 2004 she also is writing occasional pieces on new home construction for the Potomac News. She teaches sixth-grade Sunday school and serves as a Stafford County election official.

Larry Turner moved to Fredericksburg from Chicago in June 2001, following retirement from a career in college physics teaching and research. His poetry has appeared in many magazines including *Kansas Quarterly* and *Spoon River Quarterly*. Arbor Hill Press published his book of poetry *Stops on the Way to Eden and Beyond* in 1992 and his chapbook *The Girl with Blue-Eyed Parents* in 1991. He is a member of Riverside Writers, and formerly was president of the Illinois State Poetry Society and regional vice-president of the Poetry Society of Virginia. In Illinois he produced a series of cable-televisions programs, *Writers Read*.